Knowing Me, Knowing You

Knowing Me, Knowing You

The I-Sight® Way to Understand Yourself and Others

BY PAMELA ESPELAND

foreword by Tom Ritchey, President of Inscape Publishing

free spirit
PUBLISHING®
Works for kids®

Library of Congress Cataloging-in-Publication Data
Espeland, Pamela
    Knowing me, knowing you : the I-sight way to understand yourself and others / Pamela Espeland ; foreword by Tom Ritchey.
        p. cm.
    Includes bibliographical references and index.
    ISBN 1-57542-090-2 (pbk.)
    1. Typology (Psychology)—Juvenile literature. [1. Self-perception. 2. Conduct of life. 3. Interpersonal relations.] I. Title.

BF698.3.E85 2001
155.'264–dc21
                                                   2001023609

At the time of this book's publication, all facts and figures cited are the most current available; all telephone numbers, addresses, and Web site URLs are accurate and active; all publications, organizations, Web sites, and other resources exist as described in this book; and all have been verified. The author and Free Spirit Publishing make no warranty or guarantee concerning the information and materials given out by organizations or content found at Web sites, and we are not responsible for any changes that occur after this book's publication. If you find an error or believe that a resource listed here is not as described, please contact Free Spirit Publishing. Parents, teachers, and other adults: We strongly urge you to monitor children's use of the Internet.

DiSC, I-Sight, and Personal Profile System are registered trademarks of Inscape Publishing, Inc. The Myers-Briggs Type Indicator and MBTI are registered trademarks of Consulting Psychologists Press, Inc.

The "Make a fist" activity on page 63 is from *Psychology for Kids* by Jonni Kincher (Free Spirit Publishing, 1995), p. 32. The perfectionism information on page 78 is adapted from *The Gifted Kids' Survival Guide: A Teen Handbook* by Judy Galbraith and Jim Delisle (Free Spirit Publishing, 1996), p. 72. The *"I-Sight* Skills: Resolving Conflicts" chapter is adapted from *Can You Relate?* by Annie Fox (Free Spirit Publishing, 2000), pp. 232–4. All are used with permission of the publisher.

Assistant Editor: KaTrina Wentzel
Cover design: Percolator
Interior design: Marieka Heinlen
Illustrations: Jeff Tolbert

10 9 8 7 6 5 4 3 2
Printed in the United States of America

Free Spirit Publishing Inc.
217 Fifth Avenue North, Suite 200
Minneapolis, MN 55401-1299
(612) 338-2068
help4kids@freespirit.com
www.freespirit.com

DEDICATION

To John, for understanding

ACKNOWLEDGMENTS

Thanks to everyone at Inscape Publishing for teaching me about DiSC and *I-Sight,* and for their commitment to helping young people learn and use the power of DiSC in their everyday lives.

Special thanks go to Patricia Benson, Susie Moncur, Anne Neville, Anne Price, Tom Ritchey, and Laura Schauben for sharing their expertise, insights, and experiences, and for allowing me access to the wealth of DiSC and *Personal Profile System* instruments and materials published by Inscape.

CONTENTS

FOREWORD

by Tom Ritchey, President of Inscape Publishing

The main character in this book is *you!*

How could we write a book about you when we don't even know you? Good question. While we don't know you personally, we do know you share many similarities with millions of people your age. We know our human nature connects all of us in many ways.

So, while we don't know you, *Knowing Me, Knowing You* is still about you—and all the people you know, too! It's about what we have in common, how we differ, and what connects all of us. At Inscape Publishing, we have done lots of research about human behavior and how people think, feel, and act in different situations. However, in spite of all this interesting data, we don't pretend to be the experts on you. We believe *you* are the expert on how you see your world, how you react, and what you believe. We just want to help you put that information to work.

To do that, you will be able to use a cool tool called *I-Sight* to help you organize all the stuff you know about your emotions and behavior, and find answers to many of the questions you may have along the way. For example, have you ever been in a situation where a friend or classmate made you really mad? Maybe you thought to yourself, "If you were more like me, that never would have happened." *Knowing Me, Knowing You* will help you understand why others are acting the way they are and will allow you to recognize and possibly adjust your own behavior to make the most of any situation.

Understanding yourself and other people is a lifelong journey. This book is a step toward the goal of really knowing yourself and those around you. We are happy to be able to take this step with you.

Thomas Ritchey
Minneapolis, MN

INTRODUCTION

Do you ever wonder why you get along great with some people, but not so well (or not at all) with others? You're not alone—and you're not the first. Humans have been wondering about, worrying about, and working on relationships since the first groups started gathering in caves.

Do you wish you knew how to get along better with more people? That would make your life easier. It would make their lives easier, too. Imagine a world with fewer of the conflicts, confusions, and misunderstandings we all experience every day.

If someone gave you a simple tool that would help you get along better with your friends, your family, and other important people in your life, would you use it? If so, you've come to the right place.

About This Book

Knowing Me, Knowing You is based on the *I-Sight®* instrument, a proven way to understand yourself and others. *I-Sight* is short (just ten groups of phrases), easy (you rank them according to which one sounds most like you), and quick (it only takes a few minutes to complete).

So why write a whole book about it? Because a lot went into creating *I-Sight,* and you can get a lot out of it—at home, at school, with your friends, and in all of your relationships. *I-Sight* gives you insights into your thoughts, feelings, and behaviors that you'll use for a lifetime. It opens your eyes to ways in which people are different, and reasons why those differences are positive, exciting, and good for everyone—including you.

Knowing Me, Knowing You goes **behind** *I-Sight* to tell you where it came from. Learning is more than a destination. Sometimes the most interesting things happen en route to what it is you're supposed to know. If you're a curious cat, you'll enjoy reading about the people, ideas, and personality tests and typers that came before *I-Sight.*

Knowing Me, Knowing You goes **beyond** *I-Sight* to offer practical suggestions for making it part of your life.

- You'll build your self-awareness and self-esteem and become the number one expert on yourself.

- You'll recognize and develop your strengths and explore ways to overcome your limitations.

- You'll boost your people skills so you can communicate more effectively, solve problems, prevent conflicts from happening, and resolve conflicts that do happen.

- You'll discover how your behavior affects others, and how and why to flex your behavior in various situations.

- You'll learn not only to accept differences, but to welcome and celebrate differences because they make life more rich, meaningful, and fun.

The more you know about *I-Sight,* the better you'll understand it, and the more you'll get out of it.

How to Use This Book

Some people want to take *I-Sight* right away. If that's your style, go for it. You'll find it on pages 41–44. Once you take the instrument, come back to the start of the book to learn more.

Or you can begin at the beginning. If you do, you'll meet four students named Darius, Emily, Miguel, and Lian. They're very different from one another—like you and some of the people you know. Yet they're supposed to work together to complete a project assigned by their teacher, Mr. Cook. Can they do it? You'll go in and out of the classroom and see how they get along before and after *I-Sight.*

Meanwhile, you'll read about why relationships are so important, how our behavior is influenced by our perceptions, and more. You'll learn about great thinkers who lived long ago and whose ideas led up to *I-Sight.* You'll also find out about the origins of *I-Sight.* Someone didn't just make it up. It's based on years of research, testing, and experience. This means you can take it with confidence.

Throughout this book, "Reflect" activities invite you to relate what you're reading to your own experiences. You can answer the questions in your head or on paper. You may find it helpful to keep a journal while reading this book—to jot down your thoughts, any questions that occur to you, your responses to the "Reflect" activities, your ideas for making *I-Sight* part of your everyday life, and anything else that comes to mind.

Use this book in whatever way works best for you. Think about what you're reading and what it means to you personally. Talk about it with your family and friends. Maybe they'll want to take *I-Sight,* too. Then you'll share a common language that will help you all get along better than you ever thought possible.

Get in Touch

I'd love to hear how *I-Sight* works for you. What do you learn about yourself? What do you learn about other people? Does *I-Sight* make a difference in your relationships? In your life? Do you feel more positive, powerful, and successful? You can write to me at this address:

Pamela Espeland
c/o Free Spirit Publishing Inc.
217 Fifth Avenue North, Suite 200
Minneapolis, MN 55401-1299

You can also send me email or contact me through Free Spirit's Web site:

email: help4kids@freespirit.com
Web site: *www.freespirit.com*

I hope to hear from you.

Pamela Espeland
Minneapolis, Minnesota

MR. COOK'S CLASS: DARIUS

Darius has a problem. It's not the assignment his teacher just gave—to research a national monument, build a model, and report to the class. That sounds like fun.

Darius has always been interested in volcanoes, and he's heard about a national monument in Idaho called Craters of the Moon that's basically a huge, ancient lava field. He'd love to learn more about it—how old it is, how big it is, how it was formed, what it looks like. Plus it would be interesting to make a model. It would probably look like an alien landscape.

Darius's problem is the fact that this will be a group project. Mr. Cook has divided the class into fours, and Darius isn't sure he wants to work with the three other people in his group.

There's Emily, the talker. Darius worked with her on another project earlier in the school year, and she talked, talked, talked the whole time. Not that she isn't interesting. She is, and the stories she tells are entertaining. Most people really like Emily. Even Darius likes her, except when he has to work with her. She's lively and cheerful, she gets along with almost everyone, and she can talk them into doing almost anything. But she's not good with details. Darius knows that this project will be very detailed. He's worried that Emily won't do her part.

Then there's Miguel. Details aren't the issue with him. Miguel likes it when things are organized, planned, and mapped out so he knows exactly what to do every step of the way. The trouble with Miguel is that he's not very creative. Darius knows that this project will require a lot of imagination. Miguel will go along with the group, and he'll do more than his share to help and get the job done, but he won't contribute a lot of ideas.

Finally, there's Lian. Darius knows that she'll set high standards for the group, which is a good thing. She's organized, dedicated, and stays on track. But she doesn't like it when people question her work. And she tends to spend a lot of time thinking through what she's going to do, because she wants to do it right the first time. Lian might slow things down, and the group only has a limited number of hours to complete the assignment.

Darius is aware that Emily, Miguel, and Lian might have their own doubts about him. He's a take-charge kind of person, and that doesn't

4

always make him popular. He likes to set goals, solve problems, and get results. He tends to question the rules—right now he's wondering why the class has to work in assigned groups of four. Why can't he do the project on his own, or pick the people on his team? If he had his way, he'd work with Chris, Rihad, and Sarah. They'd have a good time and do an excellent job.

But Darius knows this isn't an option. Mr. Cook is already telling the groups to meet in different parts of the room and start planning their projects. Darius picks up his notebook and pen and heads for the corner table, where his group is supposed to gather. He wishes he felt better about working with Emily, Miguel, and Lian.

A VERY OLD QUESTION

It's the first day of a new school year. You walk into class, take a seat next to someone you don't know, and say hi. Minutes later, you're friends for life.

It happens. Once I went to a dinner to benefit a new center for the arts in Minneapolis, where I live. I struck up a conversation with a woman seated across the table from me. Two weeks later, we were roommates. We've been best friends for 25 years. She moved to the east coast 15 years ago, but distance doesn't matter. We email each other every day. We're friends forever.

> REFLECT: Think about one of your closest friends. Why are you friends? How long have you been friends? What makes your friendship work? What do you like most about your friend? Is there anything you don't like about him or her?

Or you walk into class, take a seat next to someone you don't know, and say hi. Minutes later, you can't stand each other.

A boy named Gregory and I had our first fight in kindergarten. We battled all the way through grade school. In sixth grade, he punched me in the mouth and chipped one of my teeth. In middle school and high school, we managed to avoid each other—mostly. I thought he was a bully. He thought I was a snob. It's not very grown-up to say this, but I hope I never see him again.

> REFLECT: Think about someone you know and don't like much—or at all. How long have you felt this way? Why do you feel this way? Is the feeling mutual? Would you like to change your relationship with this person? Why or why not?

Why Do Some People Click and others clash?

That's one of those questions that has probably been around forever. From the earliest inhabited caves to the latest reality-based TV shows, people have made and lost friends, formed and dissolved

6

alliances, established families, created communities, worked together, warred against each other, gotten together, broken up, and everything in between.

Whole fields of study—including psychology, social psychology, sociology, cultural anthropology, and social science—have grown up around the questions of how and why people do and don't get along.

Psychology: the science of mind and behavior

Social psychology: the study of how an individual's personality, attitudes, motivations, and behavior are influenced by social groups

Sociology: the science of society, social institutions, and social relationships

Cultural anthropology: a branch of anthropology that studies human culture and social structure

Social science: a branch of science that studies human society and the interpersonal relationships of individuals as members of society

Some of the best, brightest minds in human history have thought about, talked about, argued about, written about, and puzzled over human relationships. Novelists write novels about them. Poets write poems. Painters paint pictures. Sculptors sculpt. Directors make movies and TV series. (Even the most action-packed adventure has at least one friendship, family, or romance.) Composers write music about them. Singers sing about them. Rappers rap.

You made me love you
I didn't wanna do it
I didn't wanna do it
You made me want you
And all the time you knew it
I guess you always knew it

You made me happy sometimes
You made me glad
But there were times, dear,
You made me feel so bad.

From the song "You Made Me Love You (I Didn't Wanna Do It)." Words by Joe McCarthy, music by James V. Monaco (1913). Public domain.

Governments and religions make laws and set guidelines to regulate and influence how people relate to each other. Authors write books and experts give workshops on building relationships, keeping them going, and solving relationship problems. Mediators mediate when relationships are on the rocks. Counselors counsel. Parents, teachers, and other caring adults try to give kids the social skills they need to make friends, handle conflicts, and prepare for life in the human community.

REFLECT: What have the adults in your life taught you about getting along with others? Many people try to live by the Golden Rule: "Do unto others as you would have them do unto you." What are your relationship "rules"?

Yet with all of our hard work and history, we haven't figured out exactly what it takes for people to coexist in peace, harmony, and mutual respect. And when we try to explain why certain people don't get along, we often shrug and say, "Who knows? Maybe they're just too … different."

In 1991, a man named **Rodney King** was severely beaten by Los Angeles police officers. The beating was caught on videotape and aired across the U.S. During the riots that broke out in 1993 when the officers were acquitted, King begged the crowds to end the violence. "Please," he implored, "can't we all just get along?"

A Basic Need

"Cherish your human connections: your relationships with friends and family."
BARBARA BUSH

Psychologist Abraham Maslow (1908–1970) considered relationships a basic human need. Unlike other notable psychologists (such as Sigmund Freud and B.F. Skinner), who focused mostly on what's wrong with people and how to make them better, Maslow looked for the positives. He studied people like Abraham Lincoln, Eleanor Roosevelt, Albert Einstein, Jane Addams, and Frederick Douglass and concluded that human beings want to grow, love, and be loved. He believed that, given the chance, we all strive to reach our highest potential—the place where we're most creative, conscious, and wise. Relationships are key to becoming our best selves.

Some of Maslow's thinking is summarized in his Hierarchy of Needs, which he introduced in a book called *Motivation and Personality,* first published in 1954. Starting at birth, we work our way up the pyramid. Getting what we need at each level gives us the strength and motivation to reach for the next level.

"If civilization is to survive, we must cultivate the science of human relationships— the ability of all peoples, of all kinds, to live together, in the same world at peace."
FRANKLIN D. ROOSEVELT

MASLOW'S HIERARCHY OF NEEDS

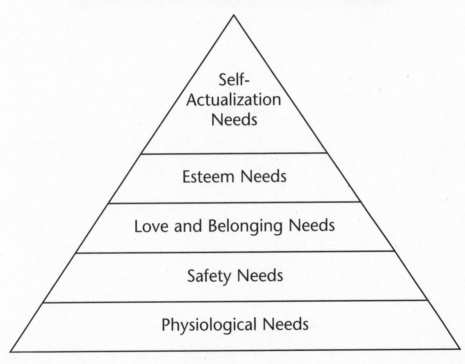

Our most basic needs are **physiological** (physical). We can't survive without water, food, sleep, exercise, and rest. Then come the **safety** needs. We must feel secure and protected, free from danger and fear. When we do, we can move up to meeting our needs for **love and belonging** by forming close, accepting, affectionate relationships with other people. From there, we can address our need for **esteem**, which includes positive self-esteem and recognition from others. Finally, we can aim for **self-actualization.** We can develop our talents, be true to our goals, and become everything we're capable of being.

"Human beings can be wonderful."
ABRAHAM MASLOW

REFLECT: Think again about your close friend and the person you don't like. Then consider these ideas. Don't accept them, reject them, or anything else right now. Just open your mind and let them in.

- We all have our own unique looks, talents, and skills. We all have our own ways of doing things and relating to others. We all have our own patterns of behavior.

- People don't (usually) do things on purpose to drive you crazy. They may annoy you simply because they behave differently than you do. Likewise, you may annoy *them* because you behave in ways they don't approve of or appreciate.

- Getting along isn't about deciding who's right and who's wrong. It's about understanding yourself and others. Understanding is where it begins.

MR. COOK'S CLASS: EMILY

Emily can't wait to start the national monument assignment. It's exactly the sort of thing she loves to do: work with other people and have fun. She looks forward to spending time with Darius, Miguel, and Lian and getting to know them all better as friends. And she's eager to tell stories about her family's visit to Montezuma Castle National Monument in Arizona.

Maybe she can even convince the group to choose that monument to report on. It's worth a try. She'll tell them about it, then ask how they'd feel about picking that as their project. But whatever they decide will be okay with her, as long as everyone agrees. The last thing she wants is for people to argue about which monument to do.

Emily is confident that Miguel and Lian will be open to her suggestion. She likes Miguel; he's calm, patient, and a good listener. He'd probably enjoy doing some of the research on the project. Emily can loan him the video and guide book she brought back from her trip. Plus she knows about a few Web sites with information about the monument. That's all stuff Miguel would want to see.

Lian could look up even more Web sites. She's a great Web researcher who always finds things other people can't. Emily knows that whatever Lian brings to the group will be checked and double-checked, because Lian likes to have her facts straight. Lian may not say much, but she has her act together, and she doesn't make mistakes.

The only person Emily's not too sure about is Darius. He'll definitely have his own ideas about the project. Emily doesn't mind hearing other ideas. In fact, she welcomes the chance. When other people talk about their thoughts and perceptions, they're usually more willing to listen to hers. Talking and listening bring people together.

But Darius can get bossy, and he doesn't like it when people don't see things his way. Emily remembers what can happen when you disagree with Darius. They worked together on a class newspaper a few months ago, and Darius got annoyed with her for talking so much.

Still, there's no point in worrying about problems before they happen. This is a new project, a new opportunity to start fresh and build friendships. Right now, Emily's too excited to let a few doubts bring her down.

11

FOUR DIMENSIONS of BEHAVIOR

About 25 years before Abraham Maslow introduced his Hierarchy of Needs, psychologist William Moulton Marston (1893–1947) was also studying "normal" people. ("Normal" as opposed to the mentally ill or criminally insane people most other psychologists studied.) Marston wanted to know how regular people felt and behaved as they interacted with the world around them. In 1928, he published his thoughts and findings in a book called *Emotions of Normal People.*

William Marston was an interesting man. A psychologist at Columbia University, he earned three degrees from Harvard, including a law degree. He invented the systolic blood-pressure test, which later led to the polygraph (lie detector). In 1943, he became a consultant for Detective Comics (now DC Comics), publisher of the *Batman* and *Superman* series.

Marston was also an early feminist. When Detective Comics head Max Gaines encouraged him to create a female comic book hero, he did, using the pen name Charles Moulton. The character's name was Diana Prince, better known as Wonder Woman. An Amazon princess and secretary to Colonel Darnell of U.S. Military Intelligence, Diana had a magic lasso she could use to force people to tell the truth. (Kind of like a lie detector.)

Wonder Woman made her debut in December 1941 in *All Star Comics* #8. The character has been in print ever since.

"Are you a 'normal' person'? Probably, for the most part, you are."
WILLIAM MARSTON

Marston spent a lot of time observing and investigating human behavior. He wanted to know what happened mentally, emotionally, and physically when an individual interacted with his or her environment. He measured things like respiration rate and galvanic skin response (a change in the skin's electrical resistance that happens in response to an emotional change). He asked people about their reactions and interviewed other psychologists about their observations. And he started seeing patterns.

REFLECT: Are you a people-watcher? If you are, what have you learned by observing how people behave in various situations? Have you noticed any patterns?

Are some people shy, while others seem more outgoing? Are some natural leaders, while others prefer to follow? Are some the life of the party, while others seem more quiet and reserved? Are some competitive, while others are cooperative? Does everyone act exactly the same when they're happy, sad, embarrassed, sleepy, scared, or surprised?

If you want, spend an hour or a day observing someone you know. Afterward, write down your observations. What did you notice? What did you learn? Do you "see" the person any differently now that you've watched him or her more carefully than usual?

Two Kinds of Perceptions

Marston theorized that people's responses to particular situations— how they feel, what they think and say and do—are based on two kinds of perceptions.

First is their perception of their *environment*. Marston believed that people perceive their environment as either **favorable** or **unfavorable**.

> "The only normal people are the ones you don't know very well."
> **JOE ANCIS**

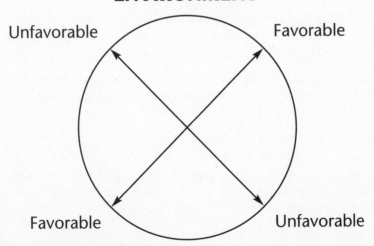

ENVIRONMENT

Unfavorable   Favorable

Favorable   Unfavorable

Example: You walk into school one morning and notice this announcement on the bulletin board:

> # LOVE MOVIES? SO DO WE! JOIN OUR CLUB.
> FIRST MEETING TUESDAY, OCTOBER 23,
> 3:15 IN THE MEDIA CENTER.
> SPONSOR: MS. ACUÑA.

You've been a serious movie fan ever since you saw the original *Star Wars* on video for the first time. The club sounds perfect for you. On Tuesday afternoon, you stroll into the media center. Then you notice that everyone else there is a grade or two ahead of you.

Do you perceive the environment as favorable or unfavorable? If you see it as **favorable**, you anticipate the fun, the warmth among people, and the successes you could have as a member of the club. You might tell yourself:

"Here's my chance to get to know some of the older kids in my school. I've seen them around and they seem okay. Plus they might know even more about movies than I do. I can learn from them. This will be great."

If you see it as **unfavorable**, you worry about the challenges, the obstacles, and the possible pitfalls you might face as a member of the club. You might think:

"Uh-oh. Everyone here is older, and they probably don't want younger kids around. Plus they're already friends with each other, and I don't know any of them very well. They'll ignore me and I'll never fit in."

Neither perception is right or more accurate than the other. They're just different. But your perception will definitely influence your behavior.

REFLECT: In general, do you perceive your environment as favorable or unfavorable? Or does that depend on where you are, who with, and what's happening? In your experience, what is the *most* favorable environment you've ever been in? The *least* favorable?

The second perception Marston identified is people's perception of *themselves* in relation to their environment. He believed that people perceive themselves as either **more powerful** or **less powerful** than their environment.

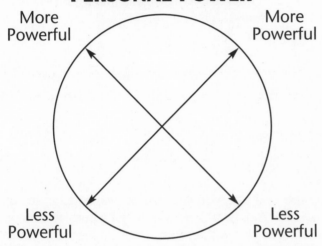

PERSONAL POWER

More
Powerful

More
Powerful

Less
Powerful

Less
Powerful

Example: You take a seat in the media center and look around. Do you perceive yourself as more powerful or less powerful than the environment of the movie club? If **more powerful**, you believe that you can have an impact, achieve your goals, and persuade others to see things your way. You might think:

> *"Okay, everyone here is older than me, but I know I have a lot to offer. If this really is a movie club and not just another clique, age won't matter. I'd like to learn more about foreign films. Maybe I can convince the group to watch some old movies by Truffaut or Kurosawa. We could even have a mini-film festival for the school."*

If you perceive yourself as **less powerful**, you think that the only way to achieve your goals is by cooperating with others and following the rules. You might tell yourself:

> *"I'll wait to see who's in charge and go along with whatever that person wants to do. I really want to be in this club, and the best way to make sure I'm welcome is to help out in any way I can. Maybe I can volunteer to come early to meetings and set up the chairs."*

"We... have the power to choose positive behaviors and responses. In that choice we change our every experience of life."
GREG ANDERSON

Again, neither perception is right or more accurate than the other. They're just different. But you will behave one way if you see yourself as powerful, another way if you don't.

REFLECT: In general, *do you perceive yourself as more powerful or less powerful than your environment? When and where have you felt the most powerful? The least powerful?*

Still not sure about the power of perception? **Imagine this:**

You're home alone. It's dark outside. The wind is gusting; a storm is on the way. You've closed the curtains and are reading a book in the family room. Except for the sound of the wind, the house is totally quiet.

Suddenly you hear a *click* against one of the windows. It stops, then again: *click click.* Your heart beats faster. Is it a burglar? You put down your book, creep across the room, peek through the curtain—and sigh with relief. It's just a tree branch blowing in the wind.

Or this:

You see your best friend in the hall between classes. She's talking with someone you don't know very well. Your friend sees you, turns back toward the other person, and they both burst out laughing. Your face burns. They must be laughing at *you.* Instead of going up to your friend, you walk away.

Later, at lunch, your friend sits down at your table. "Where did you go earlier today? Ashley told me the funniest joke, and I wanted to tell you, too. Then, all at once, you were gone. So, do you want to hear it or not?"

D, i, S, and C

In Marston's model, these two kinds of perceptions—of environment and self—work together to shape how people respond to particular situations.

- If they perceive their environment as *unfavorable* and themselves as *more powerful,* they will try to change, fix, or control their surroundings. Marston called this the **dominance (D)** dimension of behavior.

- If they perceive their environment as *favorable* and themselves as *more powerful,* they will try to bring others around to their point of view. Marston called this the **inducement (i)** dimension of behavior—later changed to **influence.**

- If they perceive their environment as *favorable* and themselves as *less powerful,* they will try to keep everything the way it is, without trying to change things too much. Marston called this the **steadiness (S)** dimension of behavior.

- If they perceive their environment as *unfavorable* and themselves as *less powerful,* they will turn inward, following clear rules and setting high standards for themselves. Marston called this the **conscientiousness (C)** dimension of behavior.

"I seem to have an awful lot of people inside me."
DAME EDITH EVANS

DIMENSIONS OF BEHAVIOR

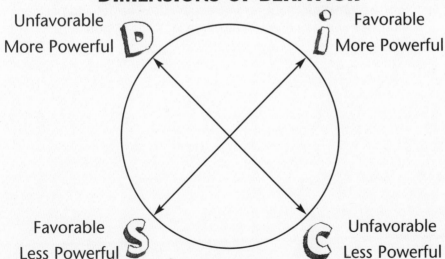

Unfavorable
More Powerful **D**

i Favorable
More Powerful

Favorable
Less Powerful **S**

C Unfavorable
Less Powerful

"oh, behave!"
AUSTIN POWERS

Later, you'll learn more about these dimensions of behavior and what they mean to you. For now, here's the most important thing you need to know: *Behaviors are not fixed, permanent, or hard-wired.* They can change. You can change them.

In other words, just because you act like a **D** in one situation doesn't mean you'll always act like a **D**, or that you are and always will be a **D**. Sometimes you'll perceive your environment as favorable, sometimes unfavorable. Sometimes you'll perceive yourself as more powerful, sometimes less powerful. The more you understand about yourself and your environment—including the people in it—the more you can flex your behavior to get what you want and need.

Based on Marston's model, we know these things about behavior:

- It's **observable.** We can see how other people behave. We're aware of our own behavior.

- It **changes** as the situation changes. We act differently with our friends than we do with strangers. We act differently at home than we do at school.

- It's **flexible** and **adaptable.** We can choose how to act and respond in various situations. We can change our behavior when that seems like the best thing to do.

- It's based on **thoughts, feelings,** and **beliefs.** We don't act in a vacuum. Our thoughts and experiences, values and beliefs influence and shape our behavior in all kinds of situations.

Notebook, pencil, pen, ruler. Miguel gathers everything he thinks he'll need for the meeting with Darius, Lian, and Emily. He adds one of the assignment sheets he created to keep track of projects he's working on. That way, he can write down what he's supposed to do and when.

Cool, calm, and organized: that's Miguel. He liked the way Mr. Cook explained their assignment. Three parts in order, one after another.

First, they'll research a national monument. Miguel thinks he might suggest the Statue of Liberty in New York City. Everyone knows what it is, but Miguel is betting that a lot of people don't know the story behind it—that it was a gift from the French people and made in France. Second, they'll build a model. The Statue of Liberty would be hard but interesting to make. They could use clay or papier-mâché. Third, they'll report to the class. Miguel won't want to be the one who actually stands up and gives the report. But he'll do his part to help the person who does.

One thing Miguel doesn't like is surprises. Another thing is change for the sake of change. He hopes that everyone will want to start by making a detailed plan. If it's a good plan, and they all work on it together, then the project should be a simple process of following the plan step-by-step. Maybe he'll ask the group if they all want copies of his assignment sheet. It works for him, and they might find it useful, too.

Miguel is worried that Darius is in their group. Darius likes to come up with new ideas and try new things. It's good that Darius is so creative, but he can also be stubborn. What if the group decides on a plan, and two weeks into the project Darius wants to head in a new direction? Darius is very persuasive, and he might be able to talk other members of the group into going along with him. If that happens, they might not complete their project on time. Plus change can be confusing, and confusion leads to tension and mistakes.

On the other hand, Lian is just the sort of person Miguel enjoys working with. She'll probably be his ally if Darius tries to make a lot of changes along the way. Lian is even more organized than Miguel. And she's totally logical, too. If they do pick the Statue of Liberty, she'll be the one who knows where and how to learn the most about it. She'll also make sure that her information is correct.

Miguel is glad that Emily is in their group. Sometimes she talks too much, but she's a lot of fun. Emily brings people together, and she always sees the bright side. She's friends with almost everyone in the class. Miguel knows that Emily will be an asset to their group. In fact, he believes that all four of them have something positive to offer— even Darius. If they can make a plan and stick to it, their project will turn out great.

MIGUEL'S ASSIGNMENT SHEET

PROJECT DESCRIPTION: _____

PROJECT DUE DATE(S): _____

TODAY'S DATE	NOTES	ASSIGNMENT OR TASK	RESOURCES (people, books, organizations, Web sites, etc.)	DATE DUE	DATE DONE

MORE FOURS: A SCENIC DETOUR

William Marston wasn't the first (or last) person to look at human behavior in fours. That started long ago with the ancient Greek thinkers.

What's the point of describing more fours? To show you how long people have been trying to figure out what makes us different. To give you a glimpse into how thinkers draw from and build on each other's ideas. Few ideas come out of nowhere. That's why it's important for people to share what they learn, discover, and know.

You may feel that this chapter is too much information for you. If so, skip it. Or you may decide you want more. You'll find suggestions for books to read and Web sites to surf. You can also check with your librarian or media center specialist.

Empedocles

Around 444 B.C., a philosopher, poet, teacher, and statesman named Empedocles (c. 490–433 B.C.) proposed that everything is made of four cosmic "roots," or elements:

1. Air
2. Earth
3. Fire
4. Water

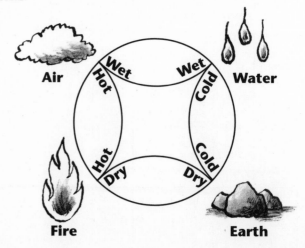

Each element has its own unique qualities. Air is hot and wet. Earth is cold and dry. Fire is hot and dry. Water is cold and wet.

In an early attempt to figure out human nature, Empedocles decided that the healthiest, smartest, most stable people are those in which all four elements are balanced.

REFLECT: We still describe people in "elemental" language today. Some are "earthy" or "down-to-earth." Others are "spacey" (airy) or "a breath of fresh air." Still others have "fiery" personalities or tempers. What about "watery" people? Maybe they're the ones who "go with the flow." Do you know someone who seems "hot" or "cold"? Or someone who has a "dry" sense of humor? Which element best describes you?

What's your sign? Are you into astrology? Then you may already know (or by now you've figured out) that the twelve signs of the zodiac relate to the four cosmic elements identified by Empedocles.

- Taurus (April 20–May 20), Virgo (August 23–September 22), and Capricorn (December 22–January 19) are **earth** signs. People born under these signs are believed to be stable, practical, patient, persistent, and dependable.

- Gemini (May 21–June 21), Libra (September 23–October 22), and Aquarius (January 20–February 18) are **air** signs. People born under these signs are believed to be curious, innovative, clever, sociable, and stimulating.

- Aries (March 21–April 19), Leo (July 23–August 22) and Sagittarius (November 22–December 21) are **fire** signs. People born under these signs are believed to be enthusiastic, confident, inspiring, independent, and generous.

- Cancer (June 22–July 22), Scorpio (October 23–November 21), and Pisces (February 19–March 20) are **water** signs. People born under these signs are believed to be sensitive, emotional, creative, supportive, and secretive.

Hippocrates

Around 400 B.C., the great physician Hippocrates (*c.* 460–377 B.C.) suggested that people's health and behavior are affected by four fluids that run through the body. He called these fluids *humors* (not the funny kind) and related them to Empedocles' four elements. The humors are:

1. Blood (related to Air)

2. Black bile (related to Earth)

3. Yellow bile (related to Fire)

4. Phlegm (related to Water)

Like Empedocles, Hippocrates believed that balance matters. Too much blood makes a person *sanguine*—lively, easy-going, sociable, carefree. Too much black bile makes a person *melancholic*—moody, quiet, thoughtful, reserved. Too much yellow bile makes a person *choleric*—restless, excitable, quick-tempered, impatient. Too much phlegm makes a person *phlegmatic*—calm, careful, even-tempered, unhurried.

REFLECT: Do you ever feel like your life is "out of balance"? What makes you feel that way? What do you do to find balance again?

Although Hippocrates and William Marston lived many centuries apart, they thought a lot alike.

- Hippocrates saw choleric people as direct, decisive leader types—like Marston's **D (Dominance)** dimension.

- Sanguine people are active and enthusiastic—like Marston's **i (Influence)** dimension.

- Phlegmatic people are stable and cooperative—like Marston's **S (Steadiness)** dimension.

- Melancholic people are meticulous and detailed—like Marston's **C (Conscientiousness)** dimension.

carl Jung

Skip ahead more than two thousand years. In 1921, Swiss psychologist Carl Jung (1876–1961), who had studied the ancient writings, described four psychological functions in his book, *Psychological Types:*

1. Thinking

2. Feeling

3. Sensing

4. Intuition

"Diversity is the most basic principle of creation. No two snowflakes, blades of grass or people are alike."
LYNN MARIA LAITALA

Jung saw Thinking and Feeling as *judging* functions—the ones we use to make decisions. Sensing and Intuition are *perceiving* functions—the ones we use to gather information.

Jung believed that our personalities depend on which of these functions is stronger than the others. He also believed that we use our strongest function in either an *extraverted* way (in public) or an *introverted* way (in private). He combined these functions and ways to describe eight psychological types: Extraverted Thinkers, Introverted Thinkers, Extraverted Feelers, Introverted Feelers, and so on.

What did Jung have to say about **relationships?** Here are three thought-provoking quotations from one of the 20th century's most influential psychologists:

- "If one does not understand a person, one tends to regard him as a fool."

- "Everything that irritates us about others can lead us to an understanding of ourselves."

- "The meeting of two personalities is like the contact of two chemical substances. If there is any reaction, both are transformed."

Myers and Briggs

In the early 1940s, Isabel Briggs Myers (1896–1980) and her mother, Katherine Cook Briggs (1875–1968), wanted to make Jung's ideas more useful and practical in everyday life. They came up with a questionnaire to help people identify their personality types. Their Myers-Briggs Type Indicator (MBTI) identifies people's preferences on four scales:

1. Extraversion (E) OR Introversion (I)

2. Sensing (S) OR Intuition (N)

3. Thinking (T) OR Feeling (F)

4. Judging (J) OR Perceiving (P)

E and I are the *energizing* preferences. Extraverts get their energy from the outside world of people, activities, and things. Introverts get their energy from their internal world of ideas, feelings, and impressions.

S and N are the *attending* (or *information gathering*) preferences. Sensers use their five senses (sight, hearing, touch, taste, smell) to determine what is real. Intuitive types use their hunches, insights, and imagination to picture what is possible.

T and F are the *deciding* preferences. Thinkers make decisions in a logical, objective way. Feelers make decisions in a personal, values-oriented way.

J and P are the *lifestyle* preferences. Judgers are planners and organizers. Perceivers are spontaneous and flexible.

The preferences combine to create sixteen different personality types—ESTJ, ENTP, INTJ, INFP, and so on.

A few years ago, a company I work for hired a consultant to administer the MBTI to its staff. When my results came back, I learned that my Reported Type (a combination of the preferences I chose) is ENTP: Extraversion, Intuition, Thinking, Perceiving. According to the description of this type, I'm outspoken, energetic, and good at solving problems ... but not so good at routine assignments. I'm interested in many things, and I like challenges. I'm happiest when I can move from one project to another. Maybe that helps to explain why I'm a writer. There's always something new to write about.

The **Myers-Briggs Type Indicator** is a very popular personality inventory. Chances are, you'll be asked to take it at some point during your life. Many schools use it in career counseling. If you want to know more about it, read:

What Type Am I? Discover Who You Really Are by Renee Baron (New York: Penguin Books, 1998). A clear, accessible, and fun introduction.

There's also a children's version of the Myers-Briggs, aimed at grades 2–8. It's called the Murphy-Meisgeier Type Indicator for Children (MMTIC). Like the Myers-Briggs, it is administered by people (including educators and counselors) who are specially trained and qualified to give it and score it.

David Keirsey

Starting in the 1950s, American psychologist David Keirsey studied the Myers-Briggs Type Indicator and earlier ways of determining what makes people tick. He came up with his own questionnaire, called the Keirsey Temperament Sorter, and identified four main temperament styles:

1. Artisan

2. Guardian

3. Rational

4. Idealist

"If I do not want what you want, please try not to tell me that my want is wrong. Or if I believe other than you, at least pause before you correct my view."
DAVID KEIRSEY

Each of these styles includes four personality types that relate to the Myers-Briggs Type Indicator. For example, Artisans include Supervisors (ESTJ), Inspectors (ISTJ), Providers (ESFJ), and Protectors (ISFJ). There are sixteen types in all.

Keirsey has also identified famous people who fit the temperament styles. Author Ernest Hemingway was an Artisan. George Washington and Mother Teresa were Guardians. Albert Einstein was a Rational. Mohandas Gandhi was an Idealist.

If you want to know more about **David Keirsey's** temperament styles, here's what to read and where to go on the Web:

Please Understand Me II: Temperament, Character, Intelligence by David Keirsey (Del Mar, CA: Prometheus Nemesis Book Co., 1998).

www.keirsey.com
Information about the temperaments, profiles of people who fit the temperaments, quotes by famous personalities, and more.

www.advisorteam.com/user/kts.asp
Go online to take the Keirsey Temperament Sorter and learn your style and type.

First problem: choose a national monument. Second: build a model. Third: tell the class about it. Lian can't wait to start the project Mr. Cook has just assigned. She loves solving problems—all kinds of problems. The more challenging, the better.

Of course, the project will take a lot of thought. Lian knows that you can't just jump into something that big and complicated. There are details to work out. Schedules to plan. Responsibilities to assign.

Lian wonders what her tasks will be. She'll wait to see what Darius, Miguel, and Emily have to say. Darius isn't much of a planner, and Emily gets distracted too easily, so Lian will look mostly to Miguel. She knows that Miguel is as organized as she is. He won't be happy until he has everything spelled out on one of his assignment sheets. That's fine with Lian.

She already has an idea of which monument to choose. Last year, during summer vacation, her family went to Fort Sumter in South Carolina. Lian found it fascinating. That's where the first battle of America's Civil War battle took place—on April 12 and 13, 1861. The Union army surrendered to the Confederates after thirty-four hours of fighting. Then the Confederates withstood a siege that lasted twenty-two months—almost two whole years. Most of the fort was ruined by the end of the siege, but you can still see a lot of the artillery, and the flags that flew over the fort.

Lian has been reading about the Civil War ever since. If Darius, Miguel, and Emily like her Fort Sumter idea, Lian can bring a wealth of knowledge and resources to the project. As far as Lian is concerned, there's no such thing as too much information.

What if everyone else in the group wants to choose a different monument? That's all right with Lian, as long as she knows exactly what her role will be. And the sooner, the better. She likes having plenty of time to plan her tasks, look at each one from all sides, and figure out the most logical way to approach it. That way, her work is correct and accurate from the start. Lian doesn't like doing things over. And she especially doesn't like it when people change their minds about what she's supposed to do, or decide to go off in another direction halfway through a project.

Darius has a tendency to ignore plans and agreements, especially when he comes up with an idea he'd rather pursue. Lian is concerned that he might make things difficult for everyone. Miguel, on the other hand, is someone who likes things to go smoothly and according to plan. Maybe, if the group pairs off for some tasks, Lian will ask to work with Miguel. Although mostly she'd like to work on her own. That's how she works best.

Emily is a fun person, always friendly and cheerful, but she tends to get off track too easily. Plus she's always asking how everyone "feels" about things. This project is about research and facts, not feelings. And Emily talks too much, which wastes everyone's time.

Lian takes her notebook and pen out of her backpack, then pauses for a moment to decide if there's anything else she needs for the group meeting. She hopes Miguel remembers to bring extra copies of his assignment sheet. That way, everyone can write down what they're supposed to do, instead of just talking about it. Less talk means more time to make plans and get started.

DiSC: MORE THAN A MODEL

William Marston developed a model that helps us understand and describe human behavior. But he never developed a way to actually *measure* behavior. He went on to other things—like creating Wonder Woman.

Many people knew about Marston's work, however. And some of them saw that his model made a lot of sense.

Focus on Behavior

When Marston studied "normal" people, he wasn't interested in learning about their values, beliefs, morals, skills, natural abilities, life experiences, education, training, genetic traits, or even their intelligence. He wanted to understand their *behavior*—what he could observe by watching them.

Marston knew that other factors can influence behavior, but he focused on what he could see. He looked at *how* people act, not the *why* or *what* behind their actions.

"Do not try to understand everything, lest you thereby be ignorant of everything."
DEMOCRITUS

> It is not speech which we should want to know:
> we should know the speaker.
> It is not things seen which we should want to know:
> we should know the seer.
> It is not sounds which we should want to know:
> we should know the hearer.
> It is not mind which we should want to know:
> we should know the thinker.
>
> The Upanishads

By watching "normal" people carefully over a period of time, Marston saw that:

- Some people try to shape their environment by overcoming opposition and challenges. These people are strong-willed, impatient, forceful, decisive, and direct. They fit the **Dominance (D)** dimension of behavior.

- Some people try to shape their environment by persuading and influencing others. These people are friendly, optimistic, outgoing, talkative, and inspiring. They fit the **Influence (i)** dimension of behavior.

- Some people don't try to shape their environment. They like things just the way they are. They cooperate with others and do their best to fit in so things will stay the same. These people are patient, practical, loyal, easy to get along with, and sensitive to the needs of others. They fit the **Steadiness (S)** dimension of behavior.

- Some people feel they can't shape their environment no matter how hard they try. So they concentrate on themselves and their own performance. They strive for quality and accuracy in their work. They are thorough, precise, analytical, and idealistic. They fit the **Conscientiousness (C)** dimension of behavior.

REFLECT: Do any of these descriptions seem to fit you? Which one? Do you see yourself in more than one description? Are you more one way sometimes, more another way at other times? As Marston might have said, that's perfectly normal. Nobody is 100 percent one way all the time. Our behavior changes as the situation changes—and as we choose to change it.

A Universal Language

Marston also saw that every "normal" person he observed showed **D, i, S,** or **C** behaviors—and sometimes all four. The fact that they had different beliefs, backgrounds, abilities, and so on didn't matter. Neither did their age, race, or gender.

"All people exhibit all four behavioral factors, in varying degrees of intensity."
WILLIAM MARSTON

In fact, Marston's dimensions fit everyone. He had created a universal language of behavior. It was a simple language that anyone could learn. It was a neutral language that didn't make value judgments. Dominance isn't better than Conscientiousness (or the other way around). Steadiness isn't right while Influence is wrong. They're just different.

People who knew Marston's work realized that his universal, simple, neutral language could help human beings understand themselves. It could also help them understand each other. When these two things happen, people get along better. They communicate more clearly. They have fewer conflicts. They can change their behavior to meet the needs of various situations. They respect, appreciate, and value individual differences.

The Personal Profile System®

Since 1928, when Marston first published his ideas, many individuals and groups have come up with ways to teach others about DiSC. One of the most popular and respected ways is the *Personal Profile System.* Developed by Inscape Publishing in Minneapolis, Minnesota, in the early 1970s, it was originally tested with 1,000 people including business executives, salespeople, engineers, clerical workers, and students.

In the early 1990s, Inscape Publishing did more research, this time with over 3,000 people. Based on the results, the company decided to revise the original *Personal Profile System.* A new version was developed and released in 1994.

People who take the *Personal Profile System* focus on a situation and respond to 28 multiple-choice questions. Then they score and interpret their own results to find out which dimension of behavior they use in a particular situation or environment. There's no outside "expert" who does the scoring and interpreting. The *Personal Profile System* assumes that people are the real experts on themselves.

So far, more than 30 million people in over 60 countries around the world have used the *Personal Profile System* to learn about themselves and others. It has been translated into 17 languages.

Who uses the *Personal Profile System?* Plumbers in New York City. Assembly-line workers in Kentucky. Roustabouts on oil rigs in the Gulf of Mexico. Police officers in Kansas. Construction crews in Florida. Electricians in Texas. People at Fortune 500 companies like IBM, AT&T, Disney, and Microsoft. In other words, all kinds of people in all kinds of jobs and places.

I-Sight®

The *Personal Profile System* was designed for adults. But why limit a good thing to grown-ups? In the early 1990s, Inscape Publishing created a version for ages 12–18. They named it *I-Sight* and tested it with nearly 1,000 young people across the USA and Canada.

In *I-Sight*, the four DiSC dimensions have been renamed. The new names are more descriptive and easier for some people to understand.

	Personal Profile System Names	*I-Sight* Names
D	Dominance	Direct & Active
i	Influence	Interested & Lively
S	Steadiness	Steady & Cooperative
C	Conscientiousness	Concerned & Correct

I-Sight has ten groups of phrases that you rank. The phrases are short and simple, so it only takes a few minutes to rank them. Like the *Personal Profile System*, *I-Sight* is self-scoring. You're in charge all the way.

MR. COOK'S CLASS: LISTEN IN

Darius, Emily, Miguel, and Lian are gathered around the corner table in Mr. Cook's room. It's their first meeting to talk about the national monument project.

Emily: This is going to be *so* much fun. We're *so* lucky to have Mr. Cook for a teacher. My friend Jessie says that in her class, Ms. O'Malley is making everyone work on their own and do written reports. That would be boring. We get to work in groups and build models. I'd *much* rather do that.

Darius: Or maybe we don't have to actually *build* a model. Maybe we could make a 3-D model on the computer instead. Or a game. You know, like *SimCity*, only ours would be *SimMonument*.

Miguel: I think we should stick to the model. That's the assignment.

Darius: Well, I know for a fact that Mr. Cook is open to new ideas, as long as they're good ideas. I'm not saying we should do a game. But we could at least think about it.

Lian: Maybe we should decide which monument to do before we talk about ways to do it.

Emily: You're right, Lian. While Mr. Cook was telling us about the assignment, I had an idea. Do you all want to hear about it?

Miguel: I do.

Lian: Me, too.

Darius: Sure.

Emily: Okay, then, here it is. Last summer, my family went to Montezuma Castle National Monument. It's in Arizona, and it's really cool. It's not really a castle. It's a five-story cliff dwelling with lots of rooms—kind of a high-rise apartment building carved right into the limestone. The Sinagua Indians lived there more than 600 years ago. You can't actually go inside, but it's *so* beautiful and mysterious. I was standing there looking up at it and imagining what it must have been like to live there. You could look out your window and see for hundreds of miles. Anyway, that's my idea. What do you all think?

Lian: I've never heard of Montezuma Castle. It sounds interesting. I could find out more about it. The National Park Service has a Web site with information about all of the monuments.

Emily: I brought back a video and a guide book. I could bring them to the next meeting, if everyone wants to see them.

Darius: Here's my idea. There's a place in Idaho called Craters of the Moon. It's not a building or a historic site. It's miles and miles of lava fields, volcanic cones, craters, and a crack in the ground called the Great Rift. It's thousands of years old. Scientists think there might even be a volcanic eruption there sometime soon.

Miguel: It might be tough to make a model of a lava field. Not impossible, but tough.

Darius: That's why I was thinking we could do something on the computer. Maybe not a game, but a computer animation. Like a flight simulator, but instead of flying in and out of airports, you're flying over lava fields.

Emily: Okay, we have two ideas now. Montezuma Castle and Craters of the Moon. Miguel or Lian, do you have an idea?

Miguel: I do, but I'm not sure I want to say. It's kind of obvious.

Emily: Let's hear it anyway. We all want to hear it, right?

Miguel: I was thinking about the Statue of Liberty. Everyone knows where it is and what it looks like, but we could find out things that everyone *doesn't* know. Like exactly how tall it is and how much it weighs. And why it was built in France. We could build a scale model and paint it to look like copper. The real one is made of copper.

Darius: Mr. Cook wants each group to pick a different monument so we're not all reporting on the same thing. Another group will probably pick the Statue of Liberty. If we pick something else, like Craters of the Moon or that Montezuma house or whatever it is, we'll have a better chance of getting the one we want.

Emily: We don't have to decide this minute what's a good idea and what isn't. The important thing is to keep coming up with ideas. We're brainstorming, and everyone should have a chance to say something. What about you, Lian?

Lian: I don't really care that much which monument we pick. I just want us all to agree so I know what I'm supposed to do.

Emily: If you have an idea, we should hear it. Then we'll have another choice to talk about.

Lian: Well, I guess I could tell you what I was thinking. I like learning about the Civil War, and my family went to Fort Sumter last summer vacation. It's in South Carolina. The first Civil War battle was fought there.

Miguel: It would be fun to build a model of a fort.

Emily: Now we have four ideas. Great! So, how can we pick one?

Darius: We could take the Statue of Liberty off our list and only have three ideas to choose from.

Emily: Why should we do that?

Darius: Because it's an easy choice. Another group is probably choosing it right now.

Miguel: Maybe we should find out for sure.

Lian: We should take our time and think carefully about which monument we want to do. We could learn more about each one before we decide. Maybe we could all do some research on our ideas and talk more at our next meeting.

Darius: We only have a month to do this project from start to finish. If we don't pick a monument today, we'll fall behind. I think we should decide during this meeting. Everyone has had a chance to talk about their ideas. Let's just vote or something.

Emily: I'm with Lian. I don't think we've talked enough. If we vote now, we'll all just vote for our own ideas. Then we're right back where we started.

Miguel: Maybe we could write all four ideas on slips of paper, put them in a hat, and pick one.

Lian: That seems fair.

Darius: I don't want to spend weeks working on a project someone pulls out of a hat. I thought the whole point was to do something we're interested in and want to learn more about.

Emily: I understand how you feel, Darius. It's like getting a grab-bag gift. That's how my family gave Christmas presents last year. Everyone picked one name and bought one present. I got a sweatshirt I'll never wear in a million years. I had to buy a present for a cousin I barely know. I spent hours at the mall and ended up getting her some soap. I felt stupid when she opened it.

Darius: Emily, maybe we could stick to choosing a monument? Or should we all talk about Christmas presents?

Lian: Come on, Darius. Emily is just trying to stay positive. At least she's not arguing.

Darius: Who's arguing? I just don't want to hear every detail of everyone's life.

Miguel: This isn't going anywhere. We need to get organized.

Lian: What if we make a plan? Today we decide to do more research. The next time we meet, we bring our research. We tell each other what we found. Everyone tries to keep an open mind. Then we vote. And then we go on from there, deciding who does what and when.

Miguel: I like that idea.

Darius: I don't, because it means we're wasting this whole meeting.

Emily: We're not wasting it, Darius. We're talking about ways to get started. We're trying to figure out how to work together.

Darius: I don't know why Mr. Cook put us on teams. He could've given us a choice to work on teams or work alone. Then we could all do what we want.

I-SIGHT: THIS IS NOT A TEST!

I-Sight helps you learn to understand yourself better, develop your strengths, and get along better with others in your life. It builds your self-awareness, self-esteem, and people skills.

I-Sight is *not* a test. There are no right or wrong answers. You can't pass or fail.

I-Sight is self-scoring. This means you can be totally honest when you answer the questions. Feedback is immediate; you don't have to wait for results. Your answers are completely confidential. You don't have to share them with anyone else unless you want to.

I-Sight reinforces things you may already know about yourself, and gives you new insights into your behavior. It also gives you perspective on how your behavior affects other people. And it gives you proven ways to interact with others more effectively, so you can prevent and resolve conflicts.

I-Sight doesn't judge you or anyone else. There are no "good" or "bad" dimensions of behavior—just *different* dimensions of behavior. We all tend to have certain strengths and limitations. Understanding ourselves is the first step toward making the most of our strengths and minimizing our less strong areas.

I-Sight is all about your point of view. The results are not based on someone else's perceptions. No one else tells you what your answers mean. You fill out the information about yourself, then decide which of the possible explanations truly describe you. You're the expert on you.

Unlike personality assessments, *I-Sight* doesn't label you. It doesn't tell you what "type" or "style" you are (or aren't). It only tells you how you tend to behave. This doesn't mean you behave one way all the time. You can flex your behavior in different situations.

To date, about 100,000 people ages 12–18 have taken *I-Sight.* If you want, you can take it now. It starts on page 41.

> Unless this is your personal copy of Knowing Me, Knowing You, please don't write in the book. Make photocopies of the I-Sight instrument and write on those instead. Even if this is your personal copy, you may want to make photocopies of the instrument. Then you can take it as often as you want. You'll also find an extra copy of I-Sight on pages 107–110.

I-SIGHT PART I: THINK ABOUT YOU

Directions: Reading from left to right, rank the phrases across each row from 4 to 1.

4 = MOST like you   2 = A LITTLE like you
3 = SOMEWHAT like you   1 = LEAST like you

Here is an example:

| 4 | want to be in charge | 2 | fun to be with | 1 | listen patiently to others | 3 | do things right the first time |

When you have finished ranking all the phrases, read down each of the four columns. Add your numbers and write the total in the space below the arrow. After you have totaled all the columns and written in each score, follow the directions in each total box.

1	want to be in charge		fun to be with		listen patiently to others		do things right the first time
2	don't like to give in		well liked by others		willing to follow orders		like to plan ahead
3	people see me as powerful		lively personality		calm and easy going		like to do things accurately
4	want to win		happy and carefree		willing to go along with others		want things to be exact
5	like to take action		like to meet people		think of others before I decide		try to do my best
6	act in a forceful way		make new friends easily		let others have what they want		want to do things well
7	do what I want		start conversations easily		like to help others out		like doing things the right way
8	will be the first to act		outgoing personality		understand others' feelings		like to know the rules
9	tend to tell others what to do		people remember me		patient with others		like being precise
10	argue with others		find it easy to meet strangers		let others lead		think things through

| If your score is LARGER THAN 22, write a **D** in the box above. | If your score is LARGER THAN 29, write an **i** in the box above. | If your score is LARGER THAN 24, write an **S** in the box above. | If your score is LARGER THAN 25, write a **C** in the box above. |

Go on to the next page →

I-SIGHT PART 2:
HOW YOU TEND TO BEHAVE

Directions: The **D, i, S,** or **C** you wrote at the bottom of Part 1 is your preferred dimension of behavior. If you wrote more than one letter, that's because you may have more than one dimension of behavior. Many people do.

Circle the letter(s) on this page that match what you wrote on Part 1. Then read the list of statements under your letter(s) to see how you might behave and what you might prefer. Put a check mark by the statements that you feel are true for you. Cross out any statements that do not fit you.

D Direct & Active

Like to solve problems and to get quick results

Tend to question the rules

Like direct answers, variety, and independence

Like being in charge of your life

Know what you want and you go after it

Like to test yourself with new challenges

S Steady & Cooperative

Like to have things organized and to have things stay the same

Tend to be patient and a good listener

Like to participate in a group rather than leading it, and like listening

Like being with people who get along

Enjoy helping people

Can be counted on to get the job done

i Interested & Lively

Like to persuade others and talk people into things

Tend to be open and talk about thoughts and feelings

Like to work with people rather than alone

Enjoy telling stories and entertaining people

Get enthusiastic about things

Don't like dealing with little details

C Concerned & Correct

Like to meet high personal standards

Tend to think a lot about things before deciding

Like to have clear rules and assignments

Enjoy figuring things out

Don't like it when people question your work

Like working with people who are organized and good at doing things

Go on to the next page →

I-SIGHT PART 3:
HOW TO GET ALONG BETTER WITH OTHERS

Directions: Review the statements for each dimension of behavior in Part 2 to better understand other people.

Remember, just as some of the statements don't seem to fit you, other people might feel that some of their statements don't fit them either.

Discover how to get along better with others by reading the statements below.

If your preferred dimension of behavior is D, remember that others may want: • time to weigh pros and cons • an explanation of your decisions • to be more friendly and open • to be more careful	**If your preferred dimension of behavior is S, remember that others may want:** • to make decisions quickly • to know your needs and wants • to challenge how things are done
If your preferred dimension of behavior is i, remember that others may want: • facts and short answers • to be more organized • to have a quieter environment	**If your preferred dimension of behavior is C, remember that others may want:** • to be direct • to talk openly about what bothers you • to have you clearly explain your rules and what you expect

Go on to the next page →

I-SIGHT PART 4: THINK MORE ABOUT IT

Now that you have read about yourself and other people, think about what you have learned.

1. What did you learn about yourself?

2. Do you agree with what you read about yourself?

3. Name two things you think are your strengths.

4. Could you recognize anyone you know when you read the other dimensions?

5. Name one situation where you could use your strengths to accomplish something.

6. What is one thing you could do to improve how you get along with someone you know?

MR. COOK'S CLASS: I-SIGHT TIME

As the groups meet to talk about the project, Mr. Cook moves around the classroom, pausing to observe, answer questions, and offer encouragement.

It's not long before he notices that some groups are having trouble getting started. One group can't agree on which monument to choose, or even how to begin the process of choosing. In another, one person seems to be making the decisions while everyone else just sits there. Another group is off track already, talking about things that aren't even related to the project.

Mr. Cook wants the project to be a team effort, and he wants each member of every group to participate, contribute, and be heard. The way things are going, that probably won't happen.

He calls the class back together, then announces that before they start the monument project, they'll spend some time learning more about themselves and each other. A tool called *I-Sight* will help them do this. Mr. Cook explains that *I-Sight* will make it easier for people to work in groups to complete their projects. *I-Sight* has other benefits, too, that the class will explore together.

It takes about forty-five minutes for everyone in the class to fill out the instrument, figure out their score, identify their preferred dimension of behavior, and discover some of what that means.

Since you've already met Darius, Emily, Miguel, and Lian and learned something about the four dimensions of behavior, it won't surprise you to learn that they each fit one of the dimensions.

- Darius fits the **Direct & Active (D)** dimension.

- Emily fits the **Interested & Lively (i)** dimension.

- Miguel fits the **Steady & Cooperative (S)** dimension.

- Lian fits the **Concerned & Correct (C)** dimension.

Remember that the four dimensions are related to our perceptions of our environment and ourselves.* These perceptions motivate us to behave in certain ways.

---

* Look back at "Four Dimensions of Behavior" on pages 12–18.

Direct & Active Darius perceives the environment as **unfavorable.** He doesn't like the fact that Mr. Cook put him in a group with three other people he didn't get to choose. But he perceives himself as **more powerful** than his environment. So he tries to change it, fix it, or control it.

People who fit the **D** dimension are motivated by power and authority. They like to be in charge. They are competitive and want to win. They easily become impatient.

Interested & Lively Emily perceives the environment as **favorable.** She loves working in groups, so she's right where she wants to be. Like Darius, Emily perceives herself as **more powerful** than her environment. So she tries to shape it by influencing others to go along with her point of view.

People who fit the **i** dimension are motivated by interacting with others and by positive recognition. They like to please others and be liked. They can be very persuasive, and their enthusiasm is catching. They don't want to get bogged down by details.

Steady & Cooperative Miguel perceives the environment as **favorable.** The group, the project, the time frame—it's all fine with him. Miguel perceives himself as **less powerful** than his environment. So he doesn't try to shape it or change it.

People who fit the **S** dimension are motivated by appreciation and cooperation. They like things to be consistent and organized. They prefer going step-by-step, following rather than leading, and taking their time. They enjoy helping others. They are threatened by change and don't like making snap decisions.

Concerned & Correct Lian perceives the environment as **unfavorable.** And she perceives herself as **less powerful** than her environment. So she turns inward and controls the only thing she can: her own performance.

People who fit the **C** dimension are motivated by quality and respect for their work. They think before making decisions. They like to figure things out for themselves—and they don't like it when other people question or criticize their work. They want rules, assignments, and expectations to be logical and clear.

As the students discover their preferred dimensions, Mr. Cook emphasizes that there are no "good" or "bad" dimensions. No dimension is right or wrong, better or worse than any other. The four dimensions are just different.

Over the next few days, Mr. Cook leads the class in activities and discussions about the preferred dimensions of behavior. Students interview each other, talk with each other, and write in their journals about what they're learning. They act out the four dimensions in role plays. At first, it's not easy. Darius has a hard time being positive, energetic, and friendly—qualities that come naturally to Emily. Emily has trouble being a good listener and paying attention to details—two of Miguel's strengths. Miguel doesn't feel comfortable making quick decisions—and develops new respect for Darius's ability to do that. Lian learns the value of helping others instead of focusing only on her own performance. Step by step, day by day, they all learn how to flex their behavior.

Mr. Cook makes buttons for the students to wear: green for **D**, red for **i**, blue for **S**, yellow for **C**. Some students wear more than one button, because they learned from *I-Sight* that they have more than one preferred dimension of behavior. He also makes pocket-sized reminder cards to help students get along better with others. One side is printed with the "How You Tend to Behave" descriptions from *I-Sight*. The other is printed with the "How to Get Along Better with Others" tips. If you'd like to make your own card (or cards), see pages 48–49.

As Mr. Cook learns more about his students and their preferred dimensions of behavior, he decides to make some changes to the original assignment. Before, all of the groups had to research a national monument, build a model, and report to the class. They still have to research a monument. But they don't have to build an actual model—unless they want to. They can use the computer to create a 3-D model (one of Darius's ideas). Or they can make a painting, a collage, a Web page, a newspaper, a book, or anything else that will allow others in the class to "see" the monument.

The reporting requirement is more flexible, too. Students don't have to get up in front of the class and give an oral report—unless they want to. They can present their project as a speech, a skit, a debate, a radio show, a video, or readings from a journal. (If the monument is a historical site, what was it like to live there or work there? If it's a park, what was it like to discover it and explore it?) Mr. Cook is also open to hearing other ideas.

Finally, Mr. Cook tells the class that part of their grade will come from them. He'll grade the actual projects, but the students in each group will grade themselves on how well they get along and work together.

48

D (Direct & Active)

You may:

- like to solve problems and to get quick results

- tend to question the rules

- like direct answers, variety, and independence

- like being in charge of your life

- know what you want and go after it

- like to test yourself with new challenges

© Inscape Publishing, Inc.

D (Direct & Active)

Others may want:

- time to weigh pros and cons

- an explanation of your decisions

- to be more friendly and open

- to be more careful

© Inscape Publishing, Inc.

i (Interested & Lively)

You may:

- like to persuade others and talk people into things

- tend to be open and talk about thoughts and feelings

- like to work with people rather than alone

- enjoy telling stories and entertaining people

- get enthusiastic about things

- not like dealing with little details

© Inscape Publishing, Inc.

i (Interested & Lively)

Others may want:

- facts and short answers

- to be more organized

- to have a quieter environment

© Inscape Publishing, Inc.

S (Steady & cooperative)

You may:

- like to have things organized and to have things stay the same
- tend to be patient and a good listener
- like to participate in a group rather than leading it, and like listening
- like being with people who get along
- enjoy helping people
- be able to be counted on to get the job done

© Inscape Publishing, Inc.

S (Steady & cooperative)

Others may want:

- to make decisions quickly
- to know your needs and wants
- to challenge how things are done

© Inscape Publishing, Inc.

C (concerned & correct)

You may:

- like to meet high personal standards
- tend to think a lot about things before deciding
- like to have clear rules and assignments
- enjoy figuring things out
- not like it when people question your work
- like working with people who are organized and good at doing things

© Inscape Publishing, Inc.

C (concerned & correct)

Others may want:

- to be direct
- to talk openly about what bothers you
- to have you clearly explain your rules and what you expect

© Inscape Publishing, Inc.

YOU-SIGHT: WHAT'S YOUR SCORE?

You've taken the *I-Sight* instrument and added up your totals for each column. What do you see?

A High Score in One Preferred Dimension of Behavior?

Example:

20 ☐	**34** i	**24** ☐	**22** ☐
If your score is LARGER THAN 22, write a **D** in the box above.	If your score is LARGER THAN 29, write an **i** in the box above.	If your score is LARGER THAN 24, write an **S** in the box above.	If your score is LARGER THAN 25, write a **C** in the box above.

When you read the "How You Tend to Behave" description for that dimension, you might think, "Yes! That sounds *exactly* like me!" You have what's called an "AHA!" experience—affirmation of something you knew or suspected all along.

Or you might think, "Wait a minute! That's not what I expected at all. I thought I was a fun, entertaining, enthusiastic **i** kind of person. But *I-Sight* says I'm a patient, helpful **S** kind of person. What's going on?"

Remember that *I-Sight* isn't a test. There are no right or wrong answers.

What if you think you should be a take-charge, problem-solving **D**, but *I-Sight* tells you something else about yourself? In our fast-paced, competitive world, isn't it better to be a **D**? Aren't **D**s the winners and leaders, movers and shakers?

Remember that no preferred dimension is better than any other. They're just different. Each dimension has its own strengths and limitations. What if the world were full of **D**s? Who would be our entertainers? Our listeners? Our planners?

Besides, *I-Sight* doesn't tell you who or what you are. It helps you understand how you *might* behave and what you *might* prefer, depending on the situation you're in. When the situation changes, your behavior changes. (More about that later.)

> "To know myself and what I need, I must learn about myself. To learn about myself, I must be open."
> **PAMELA SACKETT**

High Scores in Two Dimensions?

Example:

26 **D**	30 **i**	19 ☐	25 ☐
If your score is LARGER THAN 22, write a **D** in the box above.	If your score is LARGER THAN 29, write an **i** in the box above.	If your score is LARGER THAN 24, write an **S** in the box above.	If your score is LARGER THAN 25, write a **C** in the box above.

You may think, "Hey! How can I be two ways at once? There's something seriously wrong here!"

In fact, most people are a blend of preferred dimensions. We are all some of each, to varying degrees. In some people, one dimension is usually stronger than another. In others, two (or more) are strong.

Maybe you scored high in the both **D** and **i** dimensions. This might indicate that you're a take-charge, independent sort of person *and* you've got a lot of enthusiasm. Nothing wrong with that. Or it might indicate that you love to lead, but you're even more interested in having warm, friendly relationships with other people. Nothing wrong with that, either.

As you read the "How You Tend to Behave" descriptions and interpret your *I-Sight* score, remember that you're the expert on you. You get to accept statements you feel are true for you and reject those that don't fit you. Because *I-Sight* is self-scoring, you're the one who decides.

"The worst loneliness is not to be comfortable with yourself."
MARK TWAIN

High Scores in Three Dimensions?

Example:

17 ☐	30 **i**	27 **S**	26 **C**
If your score is LARGER THAN 22, write a **D** in the box above.	If your score is LARGER THAN 29, write an **i** in the box above.	If your score is LARGER THAN 24, write an **S** in the box above.	If your score is LARGER THAN 25, write a **C** in the box above.

It happens. Imagine that you score high in the **i**, **S**, *and* **C** dimensions. This doesn't mean you're hopelessly confused, you're wishy-washy, or you don't know yourself. It might mean that you're comfortable in a group, you're a good listener, *and* you're someone who likes to think things through before taking action.

> **Even if you score high** in more than one preferred dimension of behavior, chances are you'll score *highest* in just one. That's probably where you'll find your greatest strengths.

High Scores in All Four Dimensions?

Example:

25 D	32 i	28 S	29 C
If your score is LARGER THAN 22, write a **D** in the box above.	If your score is LARGER THAN 29, write an *i* in the box above.	If your score is LARGER THAN 24, write an **S** in the box above.	If your score is LARGER THAN 25, write a **C** in the box above.

Sorry, that's not possible. The total for all four scoring boxes can't exceed 100.

No horizontal (left-to-right) row should include more than one of each number 1–4. Each phrase should have a different ranking: 4 (MOST like you), 3 (SOMEWHAT like you), 2 (A LITTLE like you), or 1 (LEAST like you).

If you have high scores in all four dimensions, take *I-Sight* again and/or check your math.

"The ultimate mystery is one's own self."
SAMMY DAVIS JR.

No High Score in Any Dimension?

Example:

20	25	24	19
If your score is LARGER THAN 22, write a **D** in the box above.	If your score is LARGER THAN 29, write an *i* in the box above.	If your score is LARGER THAN 24, write an **S** in the box above.	If your score is LARGER THAN 25, write a **C** in the box above.

Take *I-Sight* again and/or check your math. Maybe you skipped some of the phrases. Maybe you thought that some didn't apply to you. *I-Sight* is designed so that most of the phrases apply in some way to any situation. Some may seem like a stretch, but if you think carefully about each phrase, you'll see how it fits.

focus on the Positives

A high score in any dimension shows your preferred dimension of behavior. Does a low score mean you're *not* a certain way? That seems like a logical conclusion, but with *I-Sight,* it's not.

Over the years, the research behind DiSC, on which *I-Sight* is based, has always looked on the *positive* side of all four dimensions. If you reread the statements in the "Think About You" part, you'll notice that they're positive. (Even "argue with others"—#10 in the first column—isn't negative. Arguing isn't just bickering. It's expressing an opinion, disagreeing, discussing pros and cons, stating your case, and sticking up for yourself.)

"I celebrate myself."
WALT WHITMAN

So don't assume that if you score low in the **D** dimension, you can't solve problems or take charge of your life. Or that if you score low in the **i** dimension, you can't ever be persuasive, open, or enthusiastic. Or that if you score low in the **S** dimension, you don't enjoy helping people. Or that if you score low in the **C** dimension, you're not good at figuring things out. All a low score in one dimension means is that you're higher in another dimension (or dimensions). And that may change as your situation changes. Focus on the positives.

MR. COOK'S CLASS: AFTER SCHOOL

On most days when school lets out, Darius rides the bus home. He gets off at his stop, walks three blocks to his house, and lets himself in. He's usually the first one home, so he makes himself a snack and watches TV while the house is peaceful and quiet.

Which isn't for long. In about half an hour, his two brothers, Marcus and Noah, arrive. They're both older than Darius and a lot bigger. They burst in the door, toss their backpacks on the dining-room table, and make a mess in the kitchen. Then they bounce Darius off of his comfortable spot on the sofa, grab the remote, and change the channel to something they want to watch.

Is Darius in charge? Not when his brothers are around. Do they see Darius as powerful? Ha. Does Darius argue with his brothers and tell them what to do? Hardly. In fact, Darius seems like a different person at home than when he's in school or with his friends. He loves Marcus and Noah, and he enjoys being with them. He tells them funny stories about his day. He may try to talk them into giving him the remote for a change, but he doesn't really expect them to hand it over. When they ask for his help with something, he pitches in. And when they tell him to go do his homework, he goes.

Around his brothers, Direct & Active Darius becomes Interested & Lively Darius, even Steady & Cooperative Darius. Not because he deliberately changes his behavior. He's not even aware that he's doing it. Darius has learned from years of experience what works and what doesn't when it comes to getting along with Marcus and Noah. He automatically switches into "what works" mode. That's just the way it is.

When Emily leaves school on Thursdays, she walks to a city bus stop, then rides the bus to her piano teacher's house. Emily has been taking piano lessons for about a year. At first, she didn't want to take them, but after only a few times, she was hooked. She doesn't even mind practicing the required half-hour a day. Sometimes she practices longer, and her mom has to remind her that she still has chores and homework to do.

Emily's piano teacher, Mrs. Dana, is special. Instead of starting Emily off with a lot of boring exercises and scales, she jumped right into music. The very first thing Emily learned to play was a Bach prelude. Emily already knew a little about music from singing in her church choir—she could read the notes and some other symbols—and she was thrilled to be playing real music so soon. She's still learning the basics—theory, scales, fingerings, time signatures, and so on—but Mrs. Dana always finds ways to make them interesting.

They start each lesson by going over what Emily learned last time and talking about her practice during the week. Then Mrs. Dana asks Emily to play the piece she's been practicing. When Emily makes a mistake, Mrs. Dana lets her keep playing all the way to the end. Then she waits for Emily to figure out for herself what happened and why. Afterward, Mrs. Dana shows her ways to avoid the mistake, or suggests exercises Emily can do to train her fingers not to make the mistake.

Toward the end of the lesson, the two of them plan what Emily will practice for the next several days. Mrs. Dana writes the assignment in Emily's notebook, so Emily knows exactly what she should do before they meet again. Then Mrs. Dana plays the piece for her, from start to finish. Emily sits quietly and listens carefully while Mrs. Dana plays. Her attention is totally focused on her teacher.

Both at her lesson and while she's practicing at home, Emily tries hard to do her best. She wants to be a good pianist someday—maybe even a great pianist. She sets high standards for herself. Emily is glad that she has a teacher who appreciates her hard work and effort.

Around Mrs. Dana, Interested & Lively Emily becomes Concerned & Correct Emily. She's there to listen and learn, not to entertain her teacher. Instead of being her usual lively, chatty, enthusiastic self, she's quiet and respectful, speaking only when she has a question or Mrs. Dana asks her one. Her piano lessons aren't social occasions. Emily wants to make the most of every minute with Mrs. Dana.

Miguel stores his books and backpack in his locker, grabs his gym bag, and heads to the school gym. He's involved in the after-school sports program, and for the next eight weeks they're playing his sport: basketball.

Miguel has loved basketball since he was five years old. That's when his older cousins started bringing him along to pick-up games

at their neighborhood park. He'd sit on the bench and watch them play. Afterward, they'd let him practice dribbling and shooting.

Before long, even his cousins had to admit that little Miguel had talent. The older he got and the more time he spent on the court, the more obvious his talent became. By now, he's almost a local legend. He's played on leagues at the local parks, at the Y, at the community center, and anywhere else kids gather for a game. Put a basketball in his hands, point him toward a net, and Miguel shines.

He's not very tall, but he's fast on his feet and extremely accurate. Sometimes, when he's playing new kids for the first time, they tease him about his height. That's when Miguel thinks about his hero, Tyrone "Muggsy" Bogues. While most pro players are over six feet tall, Muggsy stands just five feet three inches tall. That hasn't stopped him from playing for the Charlotte Hornets and the Toronto Raptors, wowing the NBA and fans everywhere with his red-hot passes, assists, steals, and defense-stabbing shots. A member of the NBA's top twenty career assist leaders, Muggsy may be short, but he's a giant on the court.

Miguel usually ends up as captain of whatever team he's playing on. He's known for taking charge, making quick decisions, solving problems, and getting results. He's always pushing himself, because he wants to be the best basketball player he can be. He'd like to play in the pros someday, or maybe coach a team. One way or another, basketball will always be part of his life.

In class, Miguel is Steady & Cooperative. On the court, he's Direct & Active. He's someone who can be counted on to get the job done— whether it's completing an assignment or leading his team to victory. Both dimensions of behavior are part of who he is.

Three days a week—on Monday, Wednesday, and Friday—Lian volunteers at a day-care center after school. She's been doing it for more than a year, and it's one of her favorite things.

It all started when her Girl Scout troop decided they wanted to go for a Girl Scout Silver Award, the highest award a Cadette Girl Scout can earn. They had already completed the other four requirements— earning three Interest Project awards, the Dreams to Reality Award, the Cadette Girl Scout Leadership Award, and the Cadette Girl Scout Challenge Pin. All they had left to do was to design and carry out a Silver Award Project.

Together, they decided they wanted to work with little kids. Actually, the other girls decided and Lian went along with them. At the time, she didn't have much experience with children. (Other girls in her troop have baby brothers and sisters, but Lian is an only child.) She didn't really care what project her troop chose, as long as she knew what she was supposed to do. Working with kids sounded fine to her.

They scheduled their project for the Saturday after Thanksgiving— one of the busiest shopping days of the year. From 10:00 in the morning until 6:00 at night, they baby-sat children from ages four through ten so their parents could go holiday shopping without their kids.

The project took a lot of work. First, the troop had to get permission to use a room at the community center. Then they had to plan activities, meals, and snacks, get donations of food and drinks, and decorate the room. They also had to advertise their project, take reservations from parents (so they wouldn't end up with more kids than they could handle), and arrange for adults to supervise.

Lian's job was to come up with several games the children could play, and learn how to play them so she could teach them to the other members of her troop. She spent hours in the library reading books about games, and more hours at home on her computer searching the Internet for ideas. Her troop leader suggested that she also visit a day-care center and ask the adults there about games children like to play. That's how Lian met Ms. Reilly, the head teacher at a day-care center in Lian's neighborhood.

The troop's baby-sitting day was a huge hit. They watched more than fifty kids—some for an hour or two, some for almost the whole day. At the end, Lian was exhausted but happy. The following Monday, she went back to the day-care center to thank Ms. Reilly for her help and tell her how the day had gone.

"As long as you're here," Ms. Reilly asked, "how would you like to read a story to the four-year-olds? One of my aides has the flu and couldn't come in today. Without her, the kids won't get their story."

Now Lian is a regular at the center. In addition to reading and telling stories, she sings songs, leads games, and puts on puppet shows. She's cheerful, outgoing, and very popular with the children, who can't wait for her to walk through the door. When she does, Concerned & Correct Lian becomes Interested & Lively Lian—open, enthusiastic, outgoing, and entertaining. It's a side of her that few of her friends have ever seen.

I-SIGHT SKILLS:
FLEXING YOUR BEHAVIOR

In "Mr. Cook's Class: After School," you saw Darius, Emily, Miguel, and Lian change their behavior in different situations.

Because he wants to get along with his brothers, Darius backs off from his preferred **D** dimension and shows **i** and **S** behaviors. Because she's determined to learn everything she can from her piano teacher, Emily replaces her **i** behaviors with **C** behaviors. Because he excels at basketball, Miguel is a high **D** when he's on the court. Because she loves working at the day-care center, Lian cares less about doing things right and more about relating to the children. Her **i** dimension takes charge.

"We make ourselves up as we go."
KATE GREEN

When my son Jonah was about ten years old, he went home with a friend after school. Later, I went to pick him up and asked his friend's mother how the visit had gone. "Great!" she said. "Your son is *so* helpful! I gave the boys a snack, and afterward Jonah cleared the table and put the dishes in the sink. He wanted to wash and dry them, but I told him he didn't have to. Plus he's very polite. He always says please and thank-you."

This was definitely not the Jonah I knew. But it was the Jonah who liked going to his friend's house and wanted to be invited back. (He was.)

Doing What Comes Naturally

You may have one preferred dimension of behavior, but you're really a blend of all four dimensions. (Everyone is.) You may act more like a **D** (or an **i**, **S**, or **C**) most of the time, but you draw on other behaviors in other situations. (Everyone does.) You might not do this on purpose, and you might not even realize you're doing it. But because changing your behavior helps you feel more comfortable, fit in with a group, solve a problem, avoid a conflict, or achieve something else important to you, that's what you do.

REFLECT: Look at your *I-Sight* score. What's your preferred dimension of behavior? Can you think of a situation in which you tend to behave very differently? Why do you think you change your behavior?

Right now, maybe you're telling yourself, "Other people may change their behavior, but not me. I know who I am. I'm consistent. What you see is what you get—the real me." Maybe the "real you" is more complex than you know. Find out by doing the activity on pages 60–61.

Remember: Unless this is your personal copy of *Knowing Me, Knowing You*, please don't write in the book. Photocopy pages 60–61 and write on the photocopies.

reading until *after* you do
the "Who's the Real You?" activity.
Then come back to this page and start reading again.

How many behaviors did you check? How many people you know did you list?

If you checked several behaviors and listed a lot of people, maybe you change your behavior more often than you think. If you checked a handful of behaviors and listed a few people, maybe you change your behavior less often than you could (or should) to get along better with others.

WHO'S THE REAL YOU?

Directions: 1) Read the following list of behaviors. Check the ones you sometimes do. 2) Look at the "People I Know" list on page 61. Beside each behavior you checked, write the name or names of those people who would be very surprised to see you do that.

❏ 1. Follow the rules. _____
_____

❏ 2. Be the center of attention. _____
_____

❏ 3. Finish what I start. _____
_____

❏ 4. Argue instead of giving in. _____
_____

❏ 5. Be a team player. _____
_____

❏ 6. Do things right the first time. _____
_____

❏ 7. Act upbeat and optimistic. _____
_____

❏ 8. Get organized. _____
_____

❏ 9. Get impatient. _____
_____

❏ 10. Go along with what other people want. _____
_____

❏ 11. Pay attention to details. _____
_____

❏ 12. Play to win. _____
_____

❏ 13. Act really enthusiastic about something. _____
_____

❏ 14. Get my way. _____
_____

Go on to the next page ➝

☐ 15. Help someone without being asked. _____

_____

☐ 16. Plan ahead. _____

_____

☐ 17. Tell someone how I feel. _____

_____

☐ 18. Listen without interrupting. _____

_____

☐ 19. Make a snap decision. _____

_____

☐ 20. Try to do my very best. _____

_____

☐ 21. Talk other people into doing what I want. _____

_____

☐ 22. Play fair. _____

_____

☐ 23. Say what's on my mind. _____

_____

☐ 24. Think things through. _____

People I Know

My mother	My teacher	My brother
My father	My coach	My sister
My best friend	My grandmother	Someone else I know:
My worst enemy	My grandfather	_____

Scoring

How many behaviors did I check?_____
How many people did I list?_____
NOTE: Count each time you've listed a person, even if it's the same person. For example, if you listed "My best friend" 10 times, count that as 10.

Go back to page 59

You probably suspect (or already know) that each behavior listed in "Who's the Real You?" fits a particular dimension. Look at this key, then look back at the behaviors you checked.

D (Direct & Active): 4, 9, 12, 14, 19, 23
i (Interested & Lively): 2, 5, 7, 13, 17, 21
S (Steady & Cooperative): 3, 8, 10, 15, 18, 22
C (Concerned & Correct): 1, 6, 11, 16, 20, 24

REFLECT: Do all of the behaviors you checked fit your preferred dimension? If some don't, what does that tell you about yourself?

More About Preferences

You have many preferences you may not be aware of. These are things you do without thinking, or almost without thinking. *Examples:*

- When you write with a pen or pencil, which hand do you write with?

- When you step onto an escalator, which foot do you lead with?

- Do you usually carry your backpack on your back or on one shoulder?

- Do you greet your friends with a handshake, a hug, a smile, or a high-five?

- When you do your homework, which subject do you start with?

- When you eat an Oreo cookie, do you pull it apart and attack the frosting first?

- Do you shower in the morning when you get up or in the evening before you go to bed?

- When you watch TV, do you channel surf or stick to one program?

- Is there a certain table in the school cafeteria where you always have lunch?

- When you go to a movie, do you sit near the front, near the back, or in the middle?

Make a fist with the hand you *don't* write with. Look at your fist. Is your thumb on the inside or the outside of your closed fingers?

Some people think that if your thumb is on the **inside,** this means you may be unsure of yourself and uncomfortable with other people. You may be reluctant to "take the first punch." You tend to hold your anger in.

If your thumb is on the **outside,** you may get angry easily. You probably have a strong will and are usually "on top of things."

If you use a computer with a word processor, you may be familiar with something called the preferences file. It's where you tell the computer which font you want to write in, whether the computer should check your spelling, how often the computer should remind you to save your documents, and so on. Preferences are different from commands because they're programmed in. Once you set the preferences on your computer, you don't have to think about them again—unless you decide to change them. (Or unless your computer crashes and trashes your preferences file.)

Changing your preferred behaviors involves more than a mouse click. It takes real effort. But it can be done. And there are times when it's the best thing to do.

> "People don't change their behavior unless it makes a difference for them to do so."
> **FRAN TARKENTON**

Preferences are like habits. It has been said (and behavioral studies have shown) that it takes from two to three weeks to form a new habit or break an old one. As you learn ways to flex your behavior, don't expect to master them after only one or two tries.

When Preferences Collide

Unless you live alone on a mountaintop or desert island, you interact with many people every day. You talk with each other, work together, eat meals together, study together, play together, or whatever you do with your friends, family, teachers, and other people in your life.

Most often, these are people you don't *choose* to be with. You don't choose your family. You don't choose your teachers, or the students in your classes. If you're involved in after-school groups, troops, teams, or clubs, you don't choose the leaders or the other members. You do choose your friends—or you might be part of a social group or clique where people hang out together but aren't really *friends*.

In the future, when you join the world of full-time work, you'll spend eight to ten hours a day with people you don't choose to be with. A few may become close, even lifelong friends. Others will stay acquaintances. Some you may not like at all—and they may feel the same about you. Still, you'll have to work together, get along, and be productive. The skills you're learning now will help you then.

In any group of people you find yourself in, there will be some who don't think, feel, or believe like you. They will want and value different things. Their preferred dimensions of behavior will be different from yours, so they will act differently than you in the same situation. Sometimes that won't really matter. At other times, especially when you need to work together, it will matter a lot.

If you're a high **D** paired with a high **C**, the other person's Concerned & Correct behaviors may drive you crazy. If you're a high **C** teamed with a high **D**, the other person's Direct & Active behaviors may put you on the defensive. If you're a high **i** sharing office space with a high **C**, your enthusiasm might conflict with his or her needs for quiet and solitude.

Because you've taken *I-Sight* and learned something about the dimensions, you can come up with other ways in which preferences might collide. Or maybe you know from experience what happens when someone else's behavior rubs you the wrong way—or vice versa.

There are two things you can do when you find yourself in this type of situation.

Option 1: You can stay within your preferred dimension of behavior. Use your strengths and do what you do best.

This will feel most comfortable to you, and it may be exactly what the situation requires. There are times that call for a take-charge, deciding **D**. Or an enthusiastic, persuasive **i**. Or a supportive, friendly **S**. Or a careful, quiet **C**.

Option 2: You can flex your behavior to meet the needs of the other person or the demands of the situation.

This will feel less comfortable to you. At first, it may seem false and awkward. It will take more time than behaving the way you normally do. But because you're a blend of all four dimensions, you can go beyond your usual response and draw on other behaviors. They are as much a part of you as your preferred behaviors, just not as strong or as obvious.

Imagine that the four dimensions of behavior are slider switches on a graphic equalizer—an electronic device that lets you adjust the highs and lows coming out of your stereo speakers. Maybe your personal settings look like this most of the time:

Since it's your equalizer and you control the settings, you can adjust them whenever you want. What if you're in a situation where you need to be more friendly and open, less direct and decisive? Picture yourself sliding the **D** switch *down* and the **i** switch *up*.

When you took *I-Sight,* you learned a few ways to flex your behavior.* The next part of this book describes more ways for you to think about and try. But first, you may be wondering...

Why flex?

If flexing your behavior takes work and isn't comfortable, why do it? Because it's a great way to handle difficult or challenging situations, including times when preferences collide.

When you're feeling stressed, pressured, frustrated, or angry, your behavior changes anyway. Often it changes in ways that hurt instead of help. You *react* without thinking. Your behavior makes things worse, not better.

This chart shows how people with each dimension of behavior might normally behave, how they might behave under stress, and how they might behave when they're really frustrated.

	In Normal Situations	Under Stress/ Pressure	Frustrated/ Angry
D	Take-charge Deciding	Bossy Demanding	Gives up Leaves
i	Persuading Enthusiastic	Over-sells Manipulative Attacks others' ideas	Gives in Pouts
S	Supportive Friendly	Gives in	Hurt Accusing
C	Careful Quiet	Avoids Can't decide Perfectionistic	Emotional Verbally attacks others

* See *"I-Sight* Part 3: How to Get Along Better with Others" on page 43.

When you flex your behavior, you examine the situation. You think about what might work and what might not. You consider what will make you more effective. Instead of getting carried away by the moment, you make a decision, then *act* on it.

Flexing is positive and powerful. It helps you get along better with others. It builds your relationship skills. Flexing is a strategy for success.

Don't worry. When you flex your behavior, you're not changing *who you are*. You're changing *how you act*. Flexing isn't forever. It's a one-time response to a particular situation. In a different situation, you might respond differently. You're not limited to your preferred dimension of behavior. You have choices.

I-SIGHT SKILLS:
WAYS TO FLEX

Have you ever done stretching exercises? Flexing your behavior is like stretching your muscles. The more you practice, the more comfortable the moves become and the farther you can stretch. You might think of flexing as yoga for your behavior.

If your preferred dimension of behavior is
D (Direct & Active)...

"You never really understand a person until you consider things from his point of view."
HARPER LEE

Instead of this:	Try this:
Taking charge	Holding back; getting input from others
Questioning the rules	Accepting the rules
Making quick decisions	Taking time to weigh the pros and cons; letting others decide
Being direct	Toning down your directness
Giving answers	Asking questions and really listening to what others say
Going after what you want	Finding out what others want
Speaking out	Encouraging others to speak
Aiming for fast results	Being patient
Solving a problem	Inviting others to help you solve the problem
Being independent	Being a team member
Expecting others to accept your decisions	Taking time to explain your decisions
Staying focused and on task	Being more relaxed and friendly

Acting quickly	Being more careful
Saying "I think…" or "I want…"	Asking "What do you think about…" or "How would you like to…" or "Would it be okay with you if we…"
Making demands	Making suggestions

REFLECT: Can you think of more ways to flex your behavior? What might you do to get along better with someone whose preferred dimension of behavior is i? Whose preferred dimension is S? Whose preferred dimension is C? *Tip:* Look back at page 42 for insights into how each person tends to behave.

If your preferred dimension of behavior is i (Interested & Lively)...

Instead of this:	Try this:
Trying to persuade others to see things your way	Asking others what they want and need
Talking others into going along with what you want to do	Finding out what they want to do
Talking about your thoughts and feelings	Sticking to the facts
Being super-enthusiastic	Toning down your enthusiasm; finding out what other people like
Ignoring little details	Being more organized
Wanting others to like you	Looking for things to like about them
Being the life of the party	Letting others take the spotlight
Being overly friendly	Being more reserved

"If you're in a relationship and you want to make it work, you have to be a little selfless at times."
MONTEL WILLIAMS

Focusing on the big picture	Providing more details
Cheerleading	Accepting specific responsibilities; following through
Being super-optimistic	Being realistic
Telling stories	Staying on task

REFLECT: Can you think of more ways to flex your behavior? What might you do to get along better with someone whose preferred dimension of behavior is D? Whose preferred dimension is S? Whose preferred dimension is C? Tip: Look back at page 42 for insights into how each person tends to behave.

If your preferred dimension of behavior is S (Steady & cooperative)...

Instead of this:	Try this:
Wanting everything to be organized	Loosening up a little
Trying to keep things the same	Accepting that things change, and that change can be good
Being patient	Being more assertive
Being a good listener	Talking more
Wanting everyone to get along	Understanding that it's okay when people disagree; speaking up when you disagree
Helping others	Asking for help
Being sensitive to the needs of others	Knowing what you want and need
Resisting change	Finding out the reasons for the change; keeping an open mind

Taking time to make decisions	Making decisions more quickly
Letting others have their way	Sticking up for yourself and what's important to you
Being the person everyone tells their problems to	Setting limits

REFLECT: Can you think of more ways to flex your behavior? What might you do to get along better with someone whose preferred dimension of behavior is D? Whose preferred dimension is i? Whose preferred dimension is C? *Tip:* Look back at page 42 for insights into how each person tends to behave.

If your preferred dimension of behavior is C (concerned & correct)...

Instead of this:	Try this:
Setting super-high standards for yourself	Learning what the situation or project really needs (some things require your best efforts, others don't)
Thinking things through on your own	Asking others to share their thoughts and ideas
Taking a long time to make decisions	Making decisions more quickly
Getting defensive when people question or challenge your work	Asking for constructive criticism
Wanting clear rules and assignments	Seeing the big picture
Working alone	Working with other people; asking for help

"Human beings have an inalienable right to invent themselves."
GERMAINE GREER

Expecting a lot from others	Knowing that people aren't perfect and everyone makes mistakes
Keeping your thoughts and feelings to yourself	Talking openly about your thoughts and feelings, especially when something is bothering you
Thinking you're the only one who really cares about standards	Accepting differences
Staying focused on your own performance	Noticing what other people do; being more open; talking more
Sticking to the rules	Thinking "outside the box"; being more creative
Expecting too much of yourself; being hard on yourself if you "fail"	Accepting your limitations
Being careful	Taking a risk

REFLECT: Can you think of more ways to flex your behavior? What might you do to get along better with someone whose preferred dimension of behavior is D? Whose preferred dimension is i? Whose preferred dimension is S? *Tip:* Look back at page 42 for insights into how each person tends to behave.

I-SIGHT SKILLS:
LEARNING MORE ABOUT YOU

Each preferred dimension of behavior has its own unique strengths and weaknesses. What you see as a positive, someone else might see as a negative. It all depends on your point of view.

As you learn more about your preferred dimension, you may want to take some extra time with the "Reflect" activities. Write your thoughts and ideas in a notebook or journal. You'll gain insights into yourself, and you'll have a starter list of ways to use your strengths and improve on your limitations. Read about the other dimensions, too—not just your own. This will sharpen your flexing skills (covered previously) and your people-reading skills (coming up).

"If you don't understand yourself, you don't understand anybody else."
NIKKI GIOVANNI

Some weaknesses are strengths taken to extremes. You overdo a positive behavior and suddenly it's not positive anymore. *Examples:*

- Directing **(D)** turns into bossing around.

- Persuading **(i)** becomes manipulating.

- Cooperating **(S)** becomes giving in.

- Attention to detail **(C)** turns into perfectionism.

Sometimes extreme behaviors grow out of fear. *Examples:*

- If you're a **Direct & Active D**, you may worry about losing control. So you dig in your heels and don't let others make decisions.

- If you're an **Interested & Lively i,** you may be afraid of rejection. So you go overboard trying to "make" other people like and accept you.

- If you're a **Steady & Cooperative S,** conflict may scare you. So you don't stick up for your own wants and needs.

- If you're a **Concerned & Correct C,** you may dread criticism. So you won't let yourself make a mistake or be wrong.

If your preferred dimension of behavior is
D (Direct & Active)...

The good: You're a take-charge, strong-willed, high-energy problem-solver. You enjoy competing, and you play to win. You set goals and go after them. You say what you think and mean what you say; you're honest, direct, and clear. People always know where they stand with you. You're independent, and you enjoy taking risks. Challenges don't scare you. Other people's opinions don't sway you. You keep things focused, efficient, and on task. You're not afraid to confront tough issues and situations. You can make a decision when no one else wants to. You're a leader.

REFLECT: Do you agree with this list of strengths? Is there anything you would add? Cross out? What's one situation where you could use your strengths to accomplish something?

The not-so-good: Some people might see you as stubborn, impatient, bossy, self-centered, blunt, uncaring, intolerant, insensitive, critical, demanding, and rude. At times, you seem to care only about yourself. You may have little interest in social interaction. You seem to lack empathy. You put people off. Some might even think you're a control freak.

REFLECT: Do you agree with this list of limitations? Is there anything you would add? Cross out? What's one time when you were aware of a weakness and wished you had acted differently? *Go further:* What are you afraid of? Can you see a connection between your fear(s) and your extreme behavior(s)? What can you do to cope with or even conquer your fear?

"Greatness lies not in being strong, but in the right use of strength."
HENRY WARD BEECHER

Tips for toning down your weaknesses: Try to be more patient and less direct. Learn to pace yourself better and relax. Ask more questions and really *listen* to the answers. Encourage others to express their opinions and feelings. Be warmer, more open and approachable. Take time to build relationships. Show others that you care about them. (Everyone needs other people at times—even you.) Sit back sometimes and let another person take the lead. Accept the importance of limits and certain ways of doing things, even if you disagree.

REFLECT: Can you think of other ways to improve how you get along with someone you know?

If your preferred dimension of behavior is i (Interested & Lively)...

The good: You're a people person—upbeat, lively, and fun. You love being with other people, and they love being with you. Your enthusiasm is contagious. You're an inspiration to others and a great motivator. When you describe a project or a plan, you make it sound irresistible. You're at your best when you're part of a team, and you're an excellent team player: doing your part, giving positive feedback. Even when you give negative feedback, you do it in a positive way. You're generous with your time and your praise. You're the life of the party. You keep people entertained for hours. You make friends easily. You're not afraid to talk about your feelings, and others feel comfortable being open with you. You're popular, even charismatic.

> "Nothing great was ever accomplished without enthusiasm."
> **RALPH WALDO EMERSON**

REFLECT: Do you agree with this list of strengths? Is there anything you would add? Cross out? What's one situation where you could use your strengths to accomplish something?

The not-so-good: Some people might see you as a phony—greedy for attention, always hogging the spotlight. Others might assume that you're their best friend when you're not. They may lean on you or confide in you way more than you want. Because you avoid conflict, you may seem shallow. Because you don't like dealing with little details, you may seem superficial. Some people might think that all you really care about is being popular.

REFLECT: Do you agree with this list of limitations? Is there anything you would add? Cross out? What's one time when you were aware of a weakness and wished you had acted differently? *Go further:* What are you afraid of? Can you see a connection between your fear(s) and your extreme behavior(s)? What can you do to cope with or even conquer your fear?

Tips for toning down your weaknesses: Try to be a little less eager. Talk less and listen more. Discipline yourself. Get organized and follow through on details. Accept the importance of completing work and meeting deadlines. Be aware of what others expect from you. Give shorter answers to some questions, and stick to the topic. Let others be the center of attention. Be more sensitive to their wants and needs. Accept that conflict is a normal, natural part of close relationships, and learn how to deal with it more effectively.

REFLECT: Can you think of other ways to improve how you get along with someone you know?

If your preferred dimension of behavior is S (Steady & cooperative)...

"My greatest strength is common sense."
KATHARINE HEPBURN

The good: You're the one people count on to be there, pitch in, and make things easier. You're loyal, dependable, modest, agreeable, patient, good-humored, and supportive—a great team member. When others are falling apart, you're steady as a rock. When they need a helping hand, you're there, usually without being asked. When they need a shoulder to cry on, they turn to you. You're fair, reasonable, a good listener, and tactful. People enjoy working with you because you keep things on track and running smoothly. Plus you're sensitive to the needs of others. You're easy to be with and easy to like.

REFLECT: Do you agree with this list of strengths? Is there anything you would add? Cross out? What's one situation where you could use your strengths to accomplish something?

The not-so-good: Some people might see you as passive, rigid, stubborn, and resistant to change. You may seem indecisive, hesitant, overcautious, even dull. Because you want to fit in, you may not stick up for yourself, and others may walk all over you. They may think you lack ambition and imagination. They may take you for granted and exploit your willingness to help. Your modesty may make it hard for others to give you sincere compliments.

> REFLECT: Do you agree with this list of limitations? Is there anything you would add? Cross out? What's one time when you were aware of a weakness and wished you had acted differently? Go further: What are you afraid of? Can you see a connection between your fear(s) and your extreme behavior(s)? What can you do to cope with or even conquer your fear?

Tips for toning down your weaknesses: Try being more assertive and direct. Instead of resisting change, keep an open mind. Learn to handle unexpected change. Accept the chance to grow by doing new and different things. Be a friend, but don't carry the burden of everyone else's problems. Speak up for yourself. Ask questions. Be enthusiastic. Know your own strengths and value yourself. When someone gives you a compliment, say thanks and enjoy the feeling. Instead of going along with the crowd, be your own person.

"once you can laugh at your own weaknesses, you can move forward."
GOLDIE HAWN

> REFLECT: Can you think of other ways to improve how you get along with someone you know?

If your preferred dimension of behavior is C (concerned & correct)...

The good: You're careful, conscientious, accurate, orderly, and thorough. A stickler for details. You think before you act; quick decisions aren't your style. You analyze, check, and double-check your work. You thrive under clear rules and assignments. You strive for personal excellence in everything you do, and you take pride in your work. People turn to you when something absolutely, positively has to be done right the first time. You have a reputation for reliability, high standards, and sound judgment. You're thoughtful, observant, diplomatic, and fair. You enjoy teaming up with people who share your commitment to quality, but you also work well on your own.

> REFLECT: Do you agree with this list of strengths? Is there anything you would add? Cross out? What's one situation where you could use your strengths to accomplish something?

The not-so-good: Some people might see you as stuck-up, snobbish, and intimidating. Others may resent you because your standards are so high that mere mortals can't possibly meet them. You may seem inflexible and controlling. People may feel uneasy and anxious around you—afraid of being judged, of not measuring up. You may appear weak or indecisive because you take so long to make a decision. You may be a perfectionist.

REFLECT: Do you agree with this list of limitations? Is there anything you would add? Cross out? What's one time when you were aware of a weakness and wished you had acted differently? *Go further:* What are you afraid of? Can you see a connection between your fear(s) and your extreme behavior(s)? What can you do to cope with or even conquer your fear?

Some people confuse **perfectionism** with **the pursuit of excellence.** They're not the same.

Perfectionism means thinking less of yourself because you earned a B+ instead of an A. The pursuit of excellence means thinking more of yourself for trying something new.

Perfectionism means being hard on yourself because you aren't equally talented in all sports. The pursuit of excellence means choosing some things you know you'll be good at—and others you know will be good for you or just plain fun.

Perfectionism means beating yourself up because you lost the student council election. The pursuit of excellence means congratulating yourself because you were nominated, and deciding to run again next year—if that's what you want.

If you want to learn more about perfectionism, read:

Perfectionism: What's Bad About Being Too Good? by Miriam Adderholdt, Ph.D., and Jan Goldberg (Minneapolis: Free Spirit Publishing, 1999). Explores where perfectionism comes from and provides strategies for getting it under control.

Tips for toning down your weaknesses: Try to relax and loosen up a little. Prepare, but don't overprepare. Strive for excellence, but let yourself be average on occasion. (Sometimes "good enough" really is.) Understand and accept that perfection isn't possible. Learn ways to be easier on yourself so you're free to take risks and enjoy life more. Consider taking on a greater challenge or trying something new. Give yourself permission to make mistakes. Allow yourself an occasional failure. Strike a balance in your life. Try being more open, more accepting of differences, more sensitive to the needs and feelings of the people around you. Don't expect so much from them. They—and you—are only human.

"Strength is a matter of a made-up mind."
JOHN BEECHER

REFLECT: Can you think of other ways to improve how you get along with someone you know?

It's fun to learn more about ourselves. (Aren't we the most fascinating people we know?) If you like self-tests, quizzes, experiments, and activities that give you insights into yourself, here's a book you'll enjoy:

Psychology for Kids: 40 Fun Tests That Help You Learn About Yourself by Jonni Kincher (Minneapolis: Free Spirit Publishing, 1995). Are you an extrovert or an introvert? An optimist or a pessimist? Right-brained or left-brained? Based on sound psychological concepts, this book helps you find your own answers.

And here's a book especially for girls:

Discover Yourself! The Official All About You Book of Quizzes by Lori Moore Stacy (New York: Scholastic, 2000). How close are you and your best friend? What's your style? What does your handwriting reveal? With the 25 quizzes in this book, girls can explore their emotions, learn what makes them unique, and discover how to love and accept themselves.

I-SIGHT SKILLS: PEOPLE-READING

I-Sight helped you discover your own preferred dimension of behavior. Is it possible for you to figure out someone else's dimension?

That's what William Marston did. Marston developed his DiSC model by observing human behavior. He focused on what he could see, without trying to figure out why someone was acting a certain way. He saw that people's behavior changes in different situations.

People-reading is more of an art than a science. You observe another person, talk with the person, review what you know about the person (or think you know), then make an educated guess about his or her preferred dimension. Your guess is "educated" because you've been learning about DiSC. This gives you a head start on understanding the other person—and figuring out how you can get along better with him or her.

Speaking of head starts, some scientists once believed that you could "read" people's personalities and determine their mental abilities by studying the **bumps on their heads.** This practice, called *phrenology,* was started by a 19th-century researcher named Fran Joseph Gall. He and his followers identified 37 mental and moral faculties that they thought were represented on the surface of the skull. (Destructiveness was located above the ear; Benevolence toward the front of the head; Self-Esteem toward the back.) Phrenology was hugely popular during Victorian times but has since been discredited as pseudo-science.

Try It

1. Think about someone you know. Someone you want to understand better. This might be a friend, an acquaintance, a teacher,

a coach, someone you've met at school, a family member, or anyone else in your life.

2. Look at the "People-Reading Part 1" chart on page 83. Read both sets of "Is this person…" questions at the top. Choose the one you believe best fits the person you're thinking about, then follow the arrow down. Read the descriptions in the boxes. Again, choose the one you believe best fits the person you're thinking about.

"We come.
We go.
And in
between
we try to
understand."
ROD STEIGER

CAUTION

• The chart is a *tool*, not a list of rules or right answers. Please don't use it to diagnose, label, or pigeonhole other people—especially people you don't know very well.

• Remember that behavior changes. No one acts the same way all the time.

---

3. Look at the "People-Reading Part 2" chart on page 84. If you believe that the person shows **D**, **i**, **S**, or **C** dimensions of behavior, look for that letter on the chart. Then read more about the person's behavior, what he or she might not like, and what you can do to get along better with him or her.

"We all have to
try to figure
out a better
way to get
along."
**WILMA PEARL
MANKILLER**

It's fun (but even less scientific) to guess the possible **dimensions of behavior** for people you *don't* know. Like actors, singers, sports stars, other celebrities, and people in the news. David Keirsey has identified famous people who fit his temperament styles. If you want, you can try to identify people you believe fit William Marston's four dimensions.

Make a Plan

Think about yourself and another person you want to understand better and get along with better. Then complete the "People-Reading Action Plan" on page 85.

> Remember: Unless this is your personal copy of *Knowing Me, Knowing You*, please don't write in the book. Photocopy page 85 and write on the photocopy.

Tip: Look back at *"I-Sight* Skills: Learning More About You" on pages 73–79 for more insights into the four dimensions of behavior. Look back at *"I-Sight* Skills: Ways to Flex" on pages 68–72 for more ways to get along with others.

After you try your plan, think about how and whether it's working. If you want, talk about your relationship with the other person. Get his or her opinion on what else you might do to improve your relationship.

"The most basic of all human needs is the need to understand and be understood."
RALPH NICHOLS

If you like learning more about other people, here's a book you'll enjoy:

Psychology for Kids II: 40 Fun Experiments That Help You Learn About Others by Jonni Kincher (Minneapolis: Free Spirit Publishing, 1995). Are people more logical or more emotional? Do males and females see things differently? Are we more alike or more different? Based on science and sound psychological concepts, this book makes it fun and interesting to learn more about the people in your life.

PEOPLE-READING PART 1

Is this person outgoing and active? Does the person say what he or she means?

OR

Is this person quiet and reserved? Is the person careful about what he or she says?

D — Competitive, direct, doesn't talk about feelings, wants to be in charge

S — Warm, likes cooperation, wants things to stay the same

OR

OR

i — Likes to talk, shares feelings, thinks people are most important

C — Holds back, thinks things through, wants to do things well

PEOPLE-READING PART 2

	D	i	S	C
The person's behavior	Makes quick decisions, gives short answers, takes charge	Outgoing, enthusiastic, positive, friendly	Calm, helpful, trustworthy, patient, sincere	Quiet, careful, reliable, accurate, concerned with being correct
What the person might like	Power, prestige, challenges, results, freedom	Popularity, recognition, approval, friendliness, being with others	Security, the status quo, time to adjust to changes, being with people who get along	Clear rules and expectations, time to make decisions, working alone
What the person might not like	Being controlled by others	Working alone	Conflict with others, change	Things that are unclear or messy
How to get along better	Let the person choose, be quick, don't chatter	Do people things, talk about feelings, be enthusiastic	Keep things the same, cooperate, don't get upset	Let the person be right, hold back a bit, avoid surprises, be logical

PEOPLE-READING ACTION PLAN

About me:

My highest preferred dimension of behavior is (circle one):

D   i   S   C

Here are some things I know about how I tend to behave:

_____

_____

_____

About the other person:

From what I can see, _____'s highest preferred dimension of behavior is (circle one):

D   i   S   C

Here are some things I know about how _____ tends to behave:

_____

_____

_____

Action plan:

The next time we're together, I will do this one *specific* thing to try to get along better:

_____

_____

_____

I-SIGHT SKILLS: BECOMING A GREAT COMMUNICATOR

Getting along with others takes more than understanding how *you* tend to behave. It takes more than understanding how *they* tend to behave. You need to know how to communicate with each other.

This seems like it should be a basic skill, but it's not. A lot of people just don't get it. Many of the biggest problems we humans have—conflicts, misunderstandings, hurt feelings, arguments, break-ups, even wars—happen because of poor communication.

Communication is more than trading words. Just because you're talking to someone doesn't mean you're getting your thoughts and feelings across. Just because you're listening to someone doesn't mean you're actually taking in what he or she is saying.

Whether your preferred dimension of behavior is **D**, **i**, **S**, or **C**, you'll benefit from becoming a better communicator. Here are some techniques and ideas to try.

"Good communication is as stimulating as black coffee, and just as hard to sleep after."
ANNE MORROW LINDBERGH

Listening

Do you know how to listen? (What? Huh? Could you repeat that please?) Some experts claim that people misinterpret what they hear in over 70 percent of all communications. That's because they listen *passively.*

Active listening involves specific skills. They're not hard to learn. They're easy to practice—you can start with your very next conversation. The payoff is amazing. Use active listening, and other people will start seeing you as one of the most brilliant and fascinating people they know.

"Be a good listener. Your ears will never get you in trouble."
FRANK TYGER

1. Make and keep eye contact. Don't stare the person down. Just look into his or her eyes. What if you're shy and this is hard for you to do? Try looking at the person's nose or forehead instead. It will seem as if you're looking into his or her eyes but will feel more comfortable to you.

2. Show that you're paying attention with an occasional nod, grunt, or *brief* comment. *Examples:*

    "I see what you mean."   *"I hear you."*
    "No kidding."   *"Go on."*
    "Tell me more."   *"Hmmmm."*
    "Really?"   *"Uh-huh."*

3. Ask for clarification if the other person says something you don't understand. This is not the same as challenging or interrogating him or her.

Right	**Wrong**
"I'm sorry, I don't quite understand what you're saying."	*"What on earth are you talking about?"*
"Run that by me again. I'm not sure I got it."	*"Start over. You're not making any sense."*
"Can you tell me more about that?"	*"How do you know that happened? Were you in the room? Did you see it with your own eyes? What proof do you have?"*
"What?"	*"WHAT?!?!?"*

4. Every so often, *mirror* what the other person is saying. *Example:*

    He or she says: *"I couldn't believe it! Aaron told Mrs. Jamison that I was copying his answers during the test. I mean, I would NEVER do that. I didn't even look over in his direction. Plus, if anyone was copying from anyone else, Aaron was copying from ME because he knows ZERO about biology. I was SO angry and embarrassed and now I don't know what to do!"*

    You say: *"Wow. Aaron told Mrs. Jamison you were copying his answers."*

5. Every so often, offer a *brief* comment on the other person's feelings. *Examples:*

    "You must have been surprised."
    "I can tell you were really upset."
    "I'll bet you were terrified."

"When we talk about understanding, surely it takes place only when the mind listens completely — the mind being your heart, your nerves, your ears — when you give your whole attention to it."
JIDDU KRISHNAMURTI

Basically, that's all active listening is. Paying attention. Showing by your actions and occasional words that you're paying attention. Being respectful.

Here's what active listening isn't:

- Interrupting with your own ideas, opinions, and point of view.

- Giving advice—unless the other person asks for it, in which case wait until he or she stops talking before you start.

- Tapping your feet.

- Rolling your eyes.

- Checking your watch.

- Looking around the room.

- Yawning.

- Any other behavior that indicates boredom.

- Arguing with or challenging the other person.

- Blaming or criticizing the other person.

- Watching TV, playing a video game, or surfing the Web.

- Listening to music.

- Talking on the phone to someone else.

- Thinking about what you'll say as soon as the other person stops talking. That's not listening. That's rehearsing.

REFLECT: Think back on a conversation you had recently—one that didn't go as well as you wanted. Did you really listen to the other person? Would it have made a difference if you had used active listening? What might have happened instead?

What's another way to be a better listener? Rebecca Z. Shafir, author of *The Zen of Listening,* has an interesting idea: **"Get into the movie."** Pretend you're watching a movie instead of listening to the other person. "This is a really neat way to focus," Shafir says. "At the movies our listening is magnificent. We can transfer that mindfulness at the movies to everyday conversations. You're surgically implanted in a movie. You're so engrossed that you've forgotten yourself. Forgetting yourself is a hallmark of Zen. At the movies you put your self-interest aside."

Talking

We think we know how to talk. So why do we come away from conversations feeling frustrated, dissatisfied, unheard, and misunderstood? Try these tips for talking more effectively.

Stop and *think* **before you talk.** Or, as the old saying goes, "Make sure brain is engaged before putting mouth in gear." Words have consequences. They evoke feelings. They strengthen friendships or make enemies. Words are powerful.

REFLECT: Have you had a conversation lately when you said something you wished you could take back? What did you say? How did your words affect the other person? How could you tell? What could you have said instead? Maybe it's not too late to make things right.

Say what you mean and mean what you say. Most people appreciate directness and honesty. This doesn't mean you can't also be tactful and respectful.

Watch your language. Among some of your friends, it might be all right to use colorful words. But don't assume the whole world wants to hear !@#$%, !*%#?!, and !@$*&?%!!!! on a regular basis.

"Always do what you say you are going to do. It is the glue and fiber that binds successful relationships."
JEFFRY A. TIMMONS

Use "I messages" to communicate your wants, needs, and feelings.
Here's a sample "You message":

"You make me so mad! You always want your way. You think you're the only one who's ever right. I can't talk to you because you never listen!"

Here's the basic formula for an "I message":

"I feel _____
                        (emotion)
when _____
                (this happens)
because _____ .
                (it causes this problem for me)
I want/need _____ .
                (this to happen—an idea for a solution)

And here are two sample "I messages":

"I feel pressured when you want me to make a decision right now, because I need more time to think things through. I need you to give me until tomorrow, and I'll have an answer for you then."

"I get irritated when I'm trying to study and you're telling me funny stories, because I start laughing and can't think straight. I need you to wait until after study hall to talk."

The other person has the choice of doing (or not doing) what you ask. But you've made yourself clear, and you've done it without putting him or her on the defensive.

If you feel that you're not getting through, talk more softly. Do this instead of raising your voice. The other person will have to lean in and listen harder to what you're saying. (This is a great way to keep disagreements from turning into shouting matches.)

Check your tone of voice. Are you whining? Yelling? Sneering? Mocking? Being sarcastic? Not if you really want the other person to hear you. As another old saying goes, "It's not what you say, it's how you say it."

"Nothing in life is more important than the ability to communicate effectively."
GERALD FORD

Try seeing the situation from the other person's point of view. Instead of thinking, "How can I get what I want?" think "How can we both get what we need?" This will influence your choice of words, your tone of voice, and the outcome of your conversation.

Build a feelings vocabulary. Feelings can be complicated and confusing. It's hard to tell the other person how you're feeling—a vital part of communicating your wants and needs—unless you have the words to do it. Are you *sad,* or are you miserable, devastated, worried, or heartbroken? Are you *mad,* or are you irritated, resentful, furious, or enraged? Are you *scared,* or are you shy, anxious, petrified, or in a panic? The more clearly you can explain your feelings, the more likely it is that the other person will really understand you.

To build your feelings vocabulary, listen to other people talk about their feelings. Ask adults you trust to help you explain your feelings when you're stuck. Look up feelings words in a thesaurus (the old-fashioned printed kind or the one on your computer) and find synonyms.

"Our feelings are our most genuine paths to knowledge."
AUDRE LORDE

"Timeless feelings are common to all of us."
MARTHA GRAHAM

You can also **read books about feelings.** There are many to choose from. Wander your library or bookstore (look in categories called "Health, Mind & Body," "Mind, Body & Spirit," "Wellness," and/or "Psychology"). Or check these out:

The Feelings Dictionary ... and Journal by Alexandra Delis-Abrams (Coeur d'Alene, ID: Adage Publications, 1999). Includes 650 feelings words with definitions plus 96 pages for journaling.

Stick Up for Yourself! Every Kid's Guide to Personal Power and Positive Self-Esteem by Gershen Kaufman, Ph.D., Lev Raphael, Ph.D., and Pamela Espeland (Minneapolis: Free Spirit Publishing, 1999). Includes sections on growing a feelings vocabulary, talking about your feelings, naming and claiming your feelings, and what to do when feelings are too strong to handle.

Body Language

Communication is more than words. You also "converse" with your posture, your facial expressions, and your gestures. Body language can help you or hurt you.

Positive body language shows that you're interested in the other person and the conversation. You're sincere about what you're saying, and you're sincere about wanting to know what the other person has to say. Negative body language sends different messages, from indifferent to bored, defensive to hostile.

The chart on page 93 gives you a basic body language vocabulary. Be aware that these are *guidelines,* not hard-and-fast rules. Whether your body language seems positive or negative also depends on the situation, your age, your gender, and your ethnic or cultural background.

Before you make that okay-in-America hand gesture in another country, read:

Gestures: The DO's and TABOOS of Body Language Around the World by Roger E. Axtell (New York: John Wiley & Sons, 1997). Describes more than 200 gestures used in 82 countries. Must-have know-how for the international traveler.

As yet another old saying goes, "Moderation in all things." Positive body language taken to extremes can actually be negative. If you're *too* relaxed, you might fall asleep. If you grin like a monkey, the other person might think you're making fun of him or her. If you nod like a bobble-head doll, you'll look as if you're tuning out instead of paying attention.

Tip: Before you begin a conversation you care about, think pleasant thoughts. Take a few deep breaths. Relax. Let your arms hang loose. Wiggle your hands. Shake off any tension you might be feeling.

BODY LANGUAGE	Positive	Negative
Posture	Relaxed, comfortable, at ease; facing the other person squarely; leaning toward him or her	Stiff, nervous; abrupt movements; fidgeting; turning sideways; leaning away
Facial expression	Open, friendly, smiling—or reserved, serious, and thoughtful, depending on the situation	Blank, guarded, scowling, frowning, yawning
Eye contact	Looking in the other person's eyes without staring; arching an eyebrow shows interest	Avoiding the other person's eyes; staring; squinting; looking at the person's body; looking around; rolling your eyes; pulling your eyebrows together might show doubt or anger
Arms	Relaxed, uncrossed	Folded in front of you (defensive)
Hands	Open and visible with palms up; lightly clasped in your lap	Clenched in fists; hidden; fluttering or wringing; near or covering your mouth (as if you have something to hide); playing with your hair; poking or pointing at the other person
Head	An occasional nod shows that you agree with what the other person is saying; an occasional tilt indicates interest	Holding your head perfectly still seems rigid and uncaring; shaking your head says "no" or "I don't agree with you"
Chin	Holding it up shows confidence and openness	Holding it down looks defensive and untrustworthy
Gestures	Talking with your hands shows that you're involved in the conversation, even excited about what the other person is saying. Use open, friendly gestures.	Folding your hands may seem too formal; twiddling your thumbs shows boredom. Avoid aggressive or threatening gestures.

It's **believed** that if your eyes are looking up and to the right, you're trying to recall a real memory. If your eyes are looking up and to the left, you're looking for a way out or making it up as you go along. And if your eyes typically meet the other person's less than 40 percent of the time, you may be perceived as evasive and untrustworthy.

Attitude

When you meet someone new, are you usually warm or cool? Friendly or reserved? Comfortable or uncomfortable? Curious or suspicious? Eager or hesitant? Respectful or disrespectful?

Does it depend on whether that person seems *like* you or *different from* you? What if the differences are obvious—like race, age, gender, physical abilities, or ethnic or cultural background? Does that determine how you feel and how you behave?

Of course it does. Differences make us uneasy. We're dealing with the unfamiliar. We're not sure what to say or do. We're a mix of powerful, conflicting emotions. We may feel superior or inferior. Proud or ashamed. Strong or weak. Confident or on the defensive. Courageous or fearful. Respectful or scornful. We may admire the other person or pity the other person. We may even hate the other person, even though we don't actually know him or her.

> "I believe that we should all know each other, we human carriers of so many pleasurable differences."
> **GWENDOLYN BROOKS**

In Minnesota, where I live, people are sometimes reluctant to tell each other what they really think. This is called **"Minnesota nice."** When they don't like something, some people might not come right out and say "I don't like that." Instead, they say, "Well, gosh, that's ... different." "Different" in this case does not mean *good.* "Different" means *bad.*

The French, on the other hand, have a famous saying: *"Vive la différence!"* It means "Long live the difference!" or "Hurray for the difference!" Even though I'm a Minnesotan, I prefer the French point of view. What about you?

You've learned from *I-Sight* that people behave differently. Some are Direct & Active. Some are Interested & Lively. Some are Steady & Cooperative. Some are Concerned & Correct. Most are a blend of all four preferred dimensions of behavior.

You've also learned from *I-Sight* that no dimension is right or wrong, "good" or "bad," better or worse than any other. You've read about, thought about, and maybe practiced ways to flex your behavior to get along better with people whose dimensions are different from yours.

What if you took this attitude and broadened it to include all kinds of differences? Would that affect how you perceive other people? Would it change your point of view? Would it make you more open to accepting all kinds of people?

It's worth a try. Accepting differences can lead to appreciating and celebrating differences. Celebrating, not just tolerating. You *tolerate* things you may not like but can't change. To tolerate is to put up with. To celebrate is to honor, enjoy, delight in, and be grateful for.

People are different. Not just in the ways they behave, but in too many other ways to count. You're unique and one of a kind. *So is everyone else.* When you truly understand this, you have what's called a "DUH!" experience—affirmation of something you should have known all along, and you feel kind of silly that you're just now figuring it out.

Besides, when it comes to getting along better with other people, you only have four choices:

1. You can try to change yourself. (Good luck.)

2. You can try to change them. (Impossible.)

3. You can try to surround yourself with people who are just like you. (Boring.)

4. You can decide that the world is a big place full of fascinating, sometimes challenging people, and the more different they are, the more interesting your life can be. (Duh!)

"Most people can't understand how others can blow their noses differently than they do."
IVAN TURGENEV

"I don't understand you. You don't understand me. What else do we have in common?"
ASHLEIGH BRILLIANT

The **Southern Poverty Law Center** is a nonprofit organization that combats hate, intolerance, and discrimination through education and litigation. One of its programs, called Teaching Tolerance, offers free or low-cost resources to educators at all levels. You can go on the Web and download "Tools for Tolerance: Simple Ideas for Promoting Equity and Celebrating Diversity," a 20-page document full of suggestions for you, your home, your school, your community, and more.

www.splcenter.org
The Center's Web site, with information on its many projects and programs including Teaching Tolerance.

www.tolerance.org
A special SPLC site devoted to fighting hate and teaching tolerance. Online self-tests, developed at the University of Washington and Yale University, invite you to explore your own hidden biases.

I-SIGHT SKILLS: RESOLVING CONFLICTS

In spite of your best efforts to get along with others, there will be times when conflict happens. Your *I-Sight* skills—understanding yourself and others, flexing your behavior, people-reading, communicating—will help you to avoid some conflicts, maybe many. For those you can't avoid, try this action plan.

Step 1: Calm down. It's very difficult to work out a conflict when you're really angry or upset. If you feel less-than-friendly toward the other person, spend some time by yourself before saying anything. Cool off so you'll be able to think more clearly.

Step 2: Talk to each other using "I messages" instead of "You messages." See page 90. When you focus on "I" and feelings, no one gets blamed or gets defensive. Even when the other person says something you believe is untrue, don't cut him or her off. A person's feelings, no matter what they are, are valid and deserve to be heard. As hard as it may be to sit still and keep quiet, remember that everyone in the conversation is entitled to speak without being interrupted.

Step 3: Listen effectively. Start by letting the other person speak first and explain what happened from his or her point of view. Use active listening. See pages 86–89. Listen with an open mind and an open heart.

Step 4: Speak effectively. See the tips on pages 89–91. Explain what happened from your point of view. If the other person starts to interrupt you, say something like, "Please let me finish what I'm saying, and then you can have a turn."

Step 5: Ask yourself what role you played. Instead of worrying about who's to blame, figure out how each person contributed to the conflict. Think about the other person's point of view. Ask him or her to consider yours. To ensure that all involved take responsibility for

"What people often mean by getting rid of conflict is getting rid of diversity, and it is of the utmost importance that these should not be considered the same."
M.P. FOLLETT

"You can handle anything if you think you can. Just keep your cool and your sense of humor."
SMILEY BLANTON

"Peace is not won by those who fiercely guard their differences but by those who with open minds and hearts seek out connections."
KATHERINE PATERSON

contributing to the conflict, have each person answer this question out loud: "What could I have done differently?"

> You might want to invite someone else to **mediate the discussion,** or help it go more smoothly and peacefully. This person has to be trustworthy, impartial, and fair (perhaps a counselor, an adult friend, or a peer mediator at school).

Step 6: Brainstorm peace-keeping solutions, then choose one to try. Talk later about how it worked. What compromises were made? Does everyone feel comfortable with the way the conflict has been resolved? How do you plan to handle this problem if it comes up again? Keep talking, and take turns offering ideas for handling future conflicts. Have each person answer this question out loud: "What could I do the next time something like this comes up"?

> REFLECT: Think back on a recent conflict—an argument, disagreement, or clash you had with someone you know. Would things have turned out differently if you had used this conflict resolution plan? Why or why not? Is there a conflict you're having now that you might be able to resolve by following these steps? What might you say and do? What solutions might you suggest?

"I try to take every conflict, every experience, and learn from it. Life is never dull."
OPRAH WINFREY

It takes two (or more) people to make and break a relationship—and also to patch things up. To resolve a conflict, everyone involved needs to cooperate. If you can't get this cooperation no matter how hard you try, the best you can do is to take responsibility for your part in the conflict, apologize, forgive yourself, and move on. Use what you've learned from the situation to build healthier relationships in the future.

MR. COOK'S CLASS: FINAL REPORT

While you were learning *I-Sight* skills, Darius, Emily, Miguel, and Lian were working on their national monument project.

After their first meeting, things changed for the better.

Back then, Darius was convinced that Emily would talk too much, Miguel wouldn't be creative enough, and Lian would slow things down. He wanted to do things his way. He wished he could work with three other people.

Emily was concerned that Darius would try to run the show. But she still felt positive about the project and the group.

Miguel was worried that Darius might want to make a lot of changes. To Miguel, the project was a simple matter of getting organized, making a plan, and sticking to it, with no surprises along the way.

Lian was thinking about how she'd like to work alone, if she had the choice. Like Emily and Miguel, she thought that Darius might be a problem. And she hoped that Emily wouldn't waste a lot of time talking about things that weren't related to the project.

Bossy Darius, chatty Emily, cautious Miguel, loner Lian—how would they ever get along well enough to complete a big project and present it to the class? During their first meeting, they couldn't even agree on how to start.

I-Sight helped them see how they were different. Over the next several weeks, they learned more about themselves and each other. They talked. They listened. They started realizing that their differences weren't problems, but strengths they could all draw on and use to work together.

Whenever they met, they wore the buttons Mr. Cook had made for the class. Darius wore a green **D**, Emily a red **i**, Miguel a blue **S**, and Lian a yellow **C**. When they wanted to review their dimensions of behavior, they looked at their pocket-sized reminder cards. And when one member of their group took a positive behavior too far, another (sometimes all three) would say a single word: *FLEX*. That was usually enough to get things back on track.

Their first big decision was which monument to choose. At their second project meeting, all four came prepared to tell more about their favorites.

Darius: I went on the Internet and looked up Craters of the Moon on the National Park Web site Lian told us about. It's mostly a lot of rocks and dirt and cracks in the ground. I'd still like to visit there someday and hike around, but maybe we should pick another monument for our project. Like Sunset Crater Volcano in Flagstaff, Arizona. It has an old volcano, plus some ancient cliff dwellings and pueblos.

Emily: I found out more about Montezuma Castle. A million people visit there every year, mostly in the spring. It's lucky we went in the summer, when it probably wasn't as crowded. It was really hot, though. We also drove to the Montezuma Well nearby. It's a big limestone sinkhole full of water. Anyway, Montezuma Castle looks awesome—I brought some pictures from our trip to show, and I have a video, too. It would be fun to build a model. We could do our report on how old it is, how it never should have been named Montezuma Castle—people used to think the Aztecs and their ruler, Montezuma, built it, but they didn't—and also on the Sinagua Indians who lived there. They must have been amazing builders, because the place is still almost perfect after more than 600 years.

Miguel: I spent a lot of time in the media center learning about the Statue of Liberty and looking at pictures. Lian came with me once, and she showed me this amazing Web site called American Memory that's part of the Library of Congress. She was using it to look up information about Fort Sumter, but after she taught me how to find my way around it, we both got caught up in Statue of Liberty stuff. There are videos—like a movie made by Thomas Edison—and old posters, and sheet music, and old magazine articles, and a collection called the Historic American Buildings Survey that has *hundreds* of photos.

Emily: Miguel, you sound so excited that you should go get a red **i** button to wear.

Miguel: Maybe I should. You can wear two at the same time, right? Anyway, the American Memory site is a great resource. You could probably use it to find out more about Montezuma Castle, if you want.

Lian: It was fun to look around that site with Miguel. We spent a lot of time at the computer. Mr. Alan had to come over and remind us that the bell had rung, and we'd be late for class if we didn't leave the media center right away. I thought about it afterward, and I decided that if the rest of the group wants to do the Statue of Liberty, I'm okay with that. I can learn more about Fort Sumter on my own. I probably will anyway. I can tell you more about it now, if you want to hear. But I don't really care if we pick that for our project.

Emily: Maybe we should do a monument that none of us has actually been to. Then it would be new for all of us, and more fun to learn about. I've never seen the Statue of Liberty in person. If no one else has either, I think we should just pick it and get started. Miguel, did you really find sheet music? As part of our report, we could record a song.

Darius: So three of you want the Statue of Liberty, or at least you're willing to do it. I guess I'm outnumbered. I know this isn't how I usually act, but I'm going to flex and say okay. Let's go ask Mr. Cook if another group has already picked it.

In fact, the Statue of Liberty was still available. Other groups had decided it was too obvious and had chosen something else. Darius, Emily, Miguel, and Lian had their monument.

Now their real work began. It didn't always go smoothly. Sometimes Darius got impatient. Sometimes Emily went on too long about a Liberty story she had discovered and couldn't wait to share. Sometimes Miguel was so eager to help someone else that he forgot about his own tasks and responsibilities. (That's when Emily would remind him to check his assignment sheet, where he had written down what he was supposed to do and when.) And sometimes Lian wanted everything to be too perfect.

They all learned to flex, but they also had opportunities to use their strengths. For example, they decided early on that a model of the Statue of Liberty would be hard to make. It would never look as good as the real thing, even in miniature. Since everyone in the class knew what Liberty looked like (or had a good general idea), the group didn't want to end up with something amateurish and clumsy. It was Darius who came up with a creative solution.

Darius: Maybe we don't have to make a model of the whole Statue of Liberty.

Emily: Uh-oh. Darius wants to do a *Sim Statue of Liberty*.

Darius: Ha-ha, very funny. No, I think we should make a model. Even though Mr. Cook said we didn't have to. Remember, he's open to almost anything, as long as we clear it with him first.

Lian: We all think a model would be too hard. We wouldn't get it right. It would look weird.

Darius: A *whole* model might. But what if we picked only *part* of the Statue and made a model of that?

Miguel: I don't know. That sounds too different from what we're supposed to do.

Darius: Different is good, remember? Let's brainstorm about this. If we don't do the whole Statue, which part can we do?

Emily: The torch. It's the highest part. I think we should do the torch.

Miguel: Maybe the crown. If you climb all the stairs inside, you actually look out through the openings in the crown.

Lian: The torch would be okay. So would the crown.

Darius: What about a foot?

Emily, Miguel, Lian: A *foot?*

Darius: Why not? The left foot, the one with the toes showing. The right foot is bent back and partly tucked under her robe. I'll bet you didn't know I knew so much about the Statue. I found a picture of the left foot online. There's a full-scale replica of it in the exhibit in the Statue's pedestal. Someone thought it was interesting enough to put it in the exhibit.

Lian: We could probably find a lot of really good pictures. Then we'd have plenty to work from and we'd get the details right.

Emily: We could start by doing a plaster cast of one of our own feet.

Darius: Someone with *really* big toes.

Miguel: Okay, Darius, it sounds kind of crazy, but if Mr. Cook says we can do it, we'll make a foot!

Mr. Cook laughed, then listened, then gave them the go-ahead.

What about the other group members' strengths? Emily was the one who kept everyone motivated, even during times when they were cranky and tired. She was the resident cheerleader.

One Friday after school, Darius, Miguel, and Lian all rode the bus home with her. They talked about their project for a while, did some research on Emily's computer, then moved to the family room for pizzas and a video.

Emily hadn't told them what movie they would see. It was a surprise. She had chosen an Alfred Hitchcock classic from 1942 called *Saboteur.* When Darius groaned, "This movie is so old it's in black-and-white!" Emily smiled and said, "Just watch it." They all got caught up in the story—a man is unjustly accused of sabotaging an American airplane factory during World War II, escapes from the police, then goes after the real criminal. But the best part was the ending, an action-packed scene that takes place on (where else?) the Statue of Liberty.

Miguel was the one who kept them on schedule. He made it his job to start each meeting by reviewing what the group had done so far, what they had left to do, and who was responsible for what. ("Lian: Figure out how much green paint we'll need for the foot. Darius: Buy green paint.") Miguel kept track of everyone's assignments. Emily was especially grateful.

Lian was their main researcher and champion fact-checker. She agreed to create a fact sheet about the Statue of Liberty to include in their final report. "Try to keep it under a hundred pages," Miguel teased her. "There are a *lot* of facts about the Statue of Liberty," Lian teased him back. "A hundred pages might not be enough."

As the project evolved and they started pulling their report together, they agreed to focus mostly on Liberty's early years. By then, they all knew that the Statue had undergone a major renovation in the 1980s, in time for its 100th birthday in 1986. But that was a topic all by itself. Emily suggested that they not report on anything that happened after 1900. That would be their cut-off date. When Lian heard that, she howled, so the group made an exception for her fact sheet.

For a while, they couldn't decide exactly how to give their final report. Should everyone help write it and one person read it aloud? Nobody liked that idea. Should they put on a skit? They thought about that, then learned that another group in the class would be doing a skit. One skit per class was plenty. A radio show? They didn't want to go without visuals.

Darius, Emily, Miguel, and Lian weren't arguing about what to do. They just couldn't decide. They took their problem to Mr. Cook, and he helped them come up with a solution. If they wanted, they could do a little bit of everything. They could call it a variety show. But they should try to keep it to fifteen minutes or less.

It's time. After weeks of hard work, the groups in Mr. Cook's class are giving their reports.

There are six groups. Last week, Mr. Cook told them the order they would go in. The class is hearing two reports a day for three days. Yesterday, they learned about the Petroglyph National Monument in New Mexico and the George Washington Carver National Monument in Missouri.

Today they heard about Muir Woods National Monument in California. Everyone is gathered around that group's model: a collage about the life and achievements of John Muir, the famous conservationist the park is named for. There's music playing in the background: the *Muir Woods Suite* by George Duke.

Mr. Cook gives them a few moments, then turns off the music and asks the class to take their seats. Darius, Emily, Miguel, and Lian are next.

Darius introduces their project. "You may think you know a lot about the Statue of Liberty," he begins. "It's huge. It's green. It's in New York Harbor. It's a symbol of freedom all over the world.

"We thought we knew a lot about it, too, until we started this project. We learned a lot of history, interesting facts, and stories. We found out that the Statue was made in Paris, not New York. Then it was taken apart and shipped to the United States in two hundred and fourteen crates..."

Darius does most of the talking, but Emily, Miguel, and Lian are just as busy. Miguel shows slides and photographs. Lian hands out copies of her fact sheet. (Somehow she managed to keep it to just three pages.) Emily reads the poem by Emma Lazarus that's inscribed on the Statue's pedestal ("Give me your tired, your poor...").

The class learns about the sculptor, Frederic Auguste Bartholdi, and the structural engineer, Gustave Eiffel (who also designed the Eiffel Tower). They hear how people across the United States helped raise funds for the Statue's pedestal with art exhibitions, auctions, and prize fights. And they love the model—the green foot. The real one is twenty-five feet long. The model is two and a half feet long—about one-tenth as big.

The report ends with "The Statue of Liberty Grand March," first published in 1884. It was Miguel who first found the music on the American Memory Web site. Emily studied it and realized it was too hard for her to play—but not too hard for Mrs. Dana, her piano teacher. Emily told her teacher about the monument project, showed her the music, and asked her a favor: Would she play it, and could Emily record it? Mrs. Dana said yes.

Now Emily puts the tape in the cassette player and turns up the volume. It's a rousing finale to a great report.

Later that day, Darius, Emily, Miguel, and Lian gather in the hall by Lian's locker to congratulate each other. Their big project is finally over. They're proud of themselves.

"All that's left is our grade," Lian says. "I hope Mr. Cook realizes how hard we worked."

"And how well we worked together," Miguel adds. "Remember, part of our grade is up to us. We get to decide how well we got along."

"I'd give us an A," Emily says. "If everyone agrees."

They do.

I-SIGHT PART 1: THINK ABOUT YOU

Directions: Reading from left to right, rank the phrases across each row from 4 to 1.

4 = MOST like you   2 = A LITTLE like you

3 = SOMEWHAT like you   1 = LEAST like you

Here is an example:

4 want to be in charge	**2** fun to be with	**1** listen patiently to others	**3** do things right the first time

When you have finished ranking all the phrases, read down each of the four columns. Add your numbers and write the total in the space below the arrow. After you have totaled all the columns and written in each score, follow the directions in each total box.

1	☐	want to be in charge	☐	fun to be with	☐	listen patiently to others	☐	do things right the first time
2	☐	don't like to give in	☐	well liked by others	☐	willing to follow orders	☐	like to plan ahead
3	☐	people see me as powerful	☐	lively personality	☐	calm and easy going	☐	like to do things accurately
4	☐	want to win	☐	happy and carefree	☐	willing to go along with others	☐	want things to be exact
5	☐	like to take action	☐	like to meet people	☐	think of others before I decide	☐	try to do my best
6	☐	act in a forceful way	☐	make new friends easily	☐	let others have what they want	☐	want to do things well
7	☐	do what I want	☐	start conversations easily	☐	like to help others out	☐	like doing things the right way
8	☐	will be the first to act	☐	outgoing personality	☐	understand others' feelings	☐	like to know the rules
9	☐	tend to tell others what to do	☐	people remember me	☐	patient with others	☐	like being precise
10	☐	argue with others	☐	find it easy to meet strangers	☐	let others lead	☐	think things through

↘ ☐	↘ ☐	↘ ☐	↘ ☐
If your score is LARGER THAN 22, write a **D** in the box above.	If your score is LARGER THAN 29, write an **i** in the box above.	If your score is LARGER THAN 24, write an **S** in the box above.	If your score is LARGER THAN 25, write a **C** in the box above.

Go on to the next page →

I-SIGHT PART 2:
HOW YOU TEND TO BEHAVE

Directions: The **D, i, S,** or **C** you wrote at the bottom of Part 1 is your preferred dimension of behavior. If you wrote more than one letter, that's because you may have more than one dimension of behavior. Many people do.

Circle the letter(s) on this page that match what you wrote on Part 1. Then read the list of statements under your letter(s) to see how you might behave and what you might prefer. Put a check mark by the statements that you feel are true for you. Cross out any statements that do not fit you.

D Direct & Active

Like to solve problems and to get quick results

Tend to question the rules

Like direct answers, variety, and independence

Like being in charge of your life

Know what you want and you go after it

Like to test yourself with new challenges

S Steady & Cooperative

Like to have things organized and to have things stay the same

Tend to be patient and a good listener

Like to participate in a group rather than leading it, and like listening

Like being with people who get along

Enjoy helping people

Can be counted on to get the job done

i Interested & Lively

Like to persuade others and talk people into things

Tend to be open and talk about thoughts and feelings

Like to work with people rather than alone

Enjoy telling stories and entertaining people

Get enthusiastic about things

Don't like dealing with little details

C Concerned & Correct

Like to meet high personal standards

Tend to think a lot about things before deciding

Like to have clear rules and assignments

Enjoy figuring things out

Don't like it when people question your work

Like working with people who are organized and good at doing things

Go on to the next page →

I-SIGHT PART 3:
HOW TO GET ALONG BETTER WITH OTHERS

Directions: Review the statements for each dimension of behavior in Part 2 to better understand other people.

Remember, just as some of the statements don't seem to fit you, other people might feel that some of their statements don't fit them either.

Discover how to get along better with others by reading the statements below.

If your preferred dimension of behavior is D, remember that others may want: • time to weigh pros and cons • an explanation of your decisions • to be more friendly and open • to be more careful	**If your preferred dimension of behavior is S, remember that others may want:** • to make decisions quickly • to know your needs and wants • to challenge how things are done
If your preferred dimension of behavior is i, remember that others may want: • facts and short answers • to be more organized • to have a quieter environment	**If your preferred dimension of behavior is C, remember that others may want:** • to be direct • to talk openly about what bothers you • to have you clearly explain your rules and what you expect

Go on to the next page →

I-SIGHT PART 4: THINK MORE ABOUT IT

Now that you have read about yourself and other people, think about what you have learned.

1. What did you learn about yourself?

2. Do you agree with what you read about yourself?

3. Name two things you think are your strengths.

4. Could you recognize anyone you know when you read the other dimensions?

5. Name one situation where you could use your strengths to accomplish something.

6. What is one thing you could do to improve how you get along with someone you know?

INDEX

G

Gaines, Max, 12
Gall, Fran Joseph, 80
Galvanic skin response, 12
Gemini, 23
Gestures: The DO's and TABOOS of Body Language Around the World, 92
Getting along with others, 1, 43
Ghandi, Mohandas, 27
Giovanni, Nikki, 73
Goldberg, Jan, 78
Golden Rule, the, 8
Graham, Martha, 91
Grau, Shirley Ann, 26
Green, Kate, 58
Guardian temperament style, 27

H

Habits, 63
Hemingway, Ernest, 27
Hepburn, Katharine, 76
Hierarchy of Needs, Maslow's, 9, 12
Hippocrates, 24
Human behavior. *See* Behavior, human
Humors, the four, 24

I

Idealist temperament style, 27
"I messages," 90, 97
Influence (i) dimension of behavior, 17, 24, 32, 34
Inscape Publishing, 33–34
Interested & Lively (i) dimension of behavior, 34, 42–43, 45–46, 69–70, 75, 83–84
    the good, 75
    the not-so-good, 75
Introverts, 25–26
Intuition, 25–26
Intuitive people, 26
I-Sight, 1, 34, 40–45, 50, 86, 107–110
    instrument, 41–44, 107–110
    scoring, 50–53
    skills, 58–67, 68, 73–79, 80–85, 86–96, 97–98

J

Judgers, 26
Judging functions (thinking and feeling), 25
Jung, Carl, 25–26

K

Kaufman, Gershen, 91
Keirsey, David, 27–28, 81
Keirsey Temperament Sorter, 27–28
Kincher, Jonni, 79, 82
King, Rodney, 8
Kingsley, Darwin P., 78
Krishnamurti, Jiddu, 87

L

Lao-Tzu, 33
Leaders, 13
Learning about others, 82
Learning about ourselves, 79
Leo, 23
Lian, 4, 11, 19, 29–30, 35–39, 45–47, 56–57, 99–105
Lie detector (polygraph), 12
Libra, 23
Lifestyle preferences (Myers-Briggs), 26
Limitations, 1
Lincoln, Abraham, 8
Lindbergh, Anne Morrow, 40, 86
Listening, 86–89
    active, 86, 88
    passive, 86
Long, Haniel, 80
Lorde, Audre, 91
Los Angeles police, 8

M

Mankiller, Wilma Pearl, 81
Marston, William Moulton, 12–13, 15, 17–18, 22, 24, 31, 33, 80
Marston's model of behavior, 12–18, 31–32, 80–81
Maslow, Abraham, 8–9, 12
Maslow's Hierarchy of Needs, 9, 12
MBTI. *See* Myers-Briggs Type Indicator
Melancholic people, 24
Mentally ill people, 12

ABOUT THE AUTHOR

Pamela Espeland has written and coauthored many books for teens, children, and adults including *What Kids Need to Succeed, What Teens Need to Succeed, Stick Up for Yourself!, Succeed Every Day, Making the Most of Today, Making Every Day Count,* and *Bringing Out the Best.*

ABOUT INSCAPE PUBLISHING

Inscape Publishing is an international publisher committed to developing and promoting resources that simplify complex issues and help individuals tap into their natural abilities to learn, create, and adapt for success. For nearly thirty years, Inscape Publishing profiles have helped more than 30 million people capitalize on their strengths, value their differences, and work together more effectively. For more information, visit the Web site (*www.inscapepublishing.com*).

ABOUT FREE SPIRIT PUBLISHING

Founded in 1983 by author/educator Judy Galbraith, Free Spirit is an award-winning publisher of nonfiction materials for children and teens, parents, educators, and counselors. Free Spirit specializes in SELF-HELP FOR KIDS® and SELF-HELP FOR TEENS® materials which empower young people and promote positive self-esteem through improved social and learning skills. Distributed nationally and internationally, Free Spirit materials have been translated into languages from Spanish to Slovene.

Other Great Books from Free Spirit

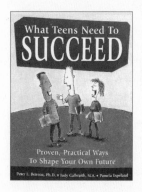

What Teens Need to Succeed
Proven, Practical Ways to Shape Your Own Future
by Peter L. Benson, Ph.D., Judy Galbraith, M.A., and Pamela Espeland
Based on a national survey, this book describes 40 developmental "assets" all teens need to succeed in life, then gives hundreds of suggestions teens can use to build assets at home, at school, in the community, in the congregation, with friends, and with youth organizations. For ages 11 & up.
$15.95; 368 pp.; softcover; illus.; 7¼" x 9¼"

Can You Relate?
Real-World Advice for Teens on Guys, Girls, Growing Up, and Getting Along
by Annie Fox, M.Ed. (also known as Hey Terra!)
Online, the author is "Terra"—a wise person who's been around long enough to know plenty, but not so long that she's forgotten what it's like to be a teen. This book brings Terra out of cyberspace and onto the printed page. Based on hundreds of emails Annie has received, it gives readers the scoop on what matters most to teens: their feelings, looks, and decisions; boyfriends and girlfriends; sex and sexuality; and much more. For ages 13 & up.
$15.95; 256 pp.; softcover; illus.; 7¼" x 9¼"

What Do You Really Want?
How to Set a Goal and Go for It! A Guide for Teens
by Beverly K. Bachel
This book is a step-by-step guide to goal-setting, written especially for teens. Each chapter includes fun and creative exercises, practical tips, words of wisdom from famous "goal-getters," real-life examples from teens, and success stories. Includes reproducibles. For ages 11 & up.
$12.95; 144 pp.; softcover; illus.; 6" x 9"

A Leader's Guide to Knowing Me, Knowing You
The I-Sight® Way to Understand Yourself and Others
by Pamela Espeland
This *Leader's Guide* supports the student book with ready-to-use lesson plans and reproducible handouts. For teachers, counselors, and youth leaders, grades 6–12.
$21.95; 112 pp.; Otabind lay-flat binding; 8½" x 11"

To place an order or to request a free catalog of SELF-HELP FOR KIDS® *and* SELF-HELP FOR TEENS® *materials, please write, call, email, or visit our Web site:*

Free Spirit Publishing Inc.
217 Fifth Avenue North • Suite 200 • Minneapolis, MN 55401-1299
toll-free 800.735.7323 • local 612.338.2068 • fax 612.337.5050
help4kids@freespirit.com • www.freespirit.com

Visit us
on the Web!

www.freespirit.com

Stop by anytime to find our Parents' Choice Approved catalog with fast, easy, secure 24-hour online ordering; "Ask Our Authors," where visitors ask questions—and authors give answers—on topics important to children, teens, parents, teachers, and others who care about kids; links to other Web sites we know and recommend; fun stuff for everyone, including quick tips and strategies from our books; and much more! Plus our site is completely searchable so you can find what you need in a hurry. Stop in and let us know what you think!

Just point and click!

new! Get the first look at our books, catch the latest news from Free Spirit, and check out our site's newest features.

contact Do you have a question for us or for one of our authors? Send us an email. Whenever possible, you'll receive a response within 48 hours.

order! Order in confidence! Our secure server uses the most sophisticated online ordering technology available. And ordering online is just one of the ways to purchase our books: you can also order by phone, fax, or regular mail. No matter which method you choose, excellent service is our goal.

1.800.735.7323 • fax 612.337.5050 • help4kids@freespirit.com